I AM Worthy

THERE IS NO LOVE
WITHOUT TRUTH

ELISHA ROSE

THE
SELF
PUBLISHING
AGENCY

Elisha Rose
I Am Worthy

Book Design | Petya Tsankova
Editor | Alison Whyte
Publishing Support | TSPA The Self Publishing Agency, Inc.

I dedicate this book to all the unlovable monsters.

> *"You can't wait until life isn't hard anymore*
> *before you decide to be happy."*

Jane Marczewski

AUTHOR'S NOTE

This story is based on my short time with Bradley. Most of my memories of our life together are painful, but I am willing to endure the discomfort of describing them if it means there is a chance to help others understand that addiction is a medical condition—not a choice.

Three weeks after Bradley's passing, I found his journal, and I decided his words should be remembered. I believe publishing what he wrote, both in his journal and in his personal notes to me that I continue to cherish, will help others to understand this was a thoughtful man who loved deeply but faced a hopeless battle.

I hope our story will provide support to people facing the same struggles. I have done my best with timelines, dialogues, and settings. I have omitted certain things Bradley wrote about and edited his words to protect certain individuals. Some names, distinguishing features, and locations have been changed to help individuals with deniability.

As author Marcella Dodge Webster reminds us, "We all color events through our own lens. Trauma makes the brain an even less reliable witness. And yet, stories have to be told."

Bradley wanted to be heard, and I know he wanted our story told.

You don't have to be smart to write a book.
You just have to have something to say.
Bradley

(A note Bradley left for me on my desk, March 2017)

PROLOGUE

I can't move. I am so cold. I feel the tears sting, forming salty pools in the corners of my eyes. They are so raw and swollen, I can barely see through them. I smell of rust, the odour lingering. I see the broken glass and the blood oozing from my knuckles, but I don't feel the pain. I replay his words over and over in my head.

"You are a selfish and vain woman!"

"Please Bradley!" I begged. "You are sick, and you need help!"

This was my last desperate attempt to reach behind the mask of a very ill man. He disregarded my plea and before he sped away in his truck filled with all that was left of his belongings, he yelled, "If I ever leave again, I am never coming back!"

These words hit hard and heavy. I can't escape them or the pain I have endured. I walked away shaking with a rage I have never before felt. I entered my house and closed the door behind me.

"Ah!" I screamed as loud as I possibly could.

"Ahhhh!" I shrieked again, but somehow even louder.

I turned into a monster destroying everything in my path.

I threw dishes against the wall, and they shattered instantly on contact. I massacred unopened packages of food. Coffee grounds, sugar, and broken eggs covered the floor as I stomped my way towards the pictures on the wall. I punched through the glass covering my children's faces, tossing what was left of the frame aside. I left a trail of destruction in every room, punching walls and kicking in doors. Finally, I collapsed on the cold tile floor in the bathroom and let the tears flow; they quenched the fire and rage, leaving me cold, crippled, and lifeless.

Time is no longer a factor, and I feel nothing. I know I can't take the pain any longer; I can't bear it another day. That's when I see the bottle.

"Do you want the pain to stop?" I ask myself.

For a moment, I forget myself as I consider taking my own life. Out of breath and with tears falling onto the blood-covered floor, I move closer until I am within reach of the bottle of opioids.

But then I freeze, paralyzed in place, and unable to move my body. I feel a sense of warmth on my cheek. I dare not move. A light is shining through the bathroom window and encircling my whole body. My cheek is burning so intensely and then I hear it.

"I will take the pain. You are worthy of me!"

If you want the pain to stop, you don't have to take your life. You have to take your life back.

No matter what life throws at us
we will always find our happily ever after.
All my love, Bradley

(From Bradley's birthday card to me, September 2017)

ONE

I grew up in the country, outside Prince George, British Columbia—north of the John Hart Highway on Chief Lake Road. I was constantly told I was a "Hart girl." Apparently, we had a bad reputation amongst other high schools that were closer to downtown Prince George. I never really put a lot of thought into these rumours until I witnessed a fight myself. I will never forget my first week of high school at Kelly Road Secondary. A huge fight broke out in the parking lot. You could tell who was who by the clothing: Kelly Road guys were hicks dressed in blue jean jackets, pants to match, cowboy boots, and baseball caps. I saw the smallest hick of the group smash a kid's head through a truck window and continue swinging. I had never seen a fight before. I was in complete shock. Starstruck. That little punk didn't have a mark on him.

Hart girls were dirty fighters—they didn't fight fair; they fought to win no matter the cost. Guys from our high school would volunteer to police the fights as things would escalate so quickly. I wasn't a fighter—not even close. Don't get me wrong, I was strong. Growing up in the country made me that way. I am the oldest sibling and honestly my dad treated me like a son when it came to running the home. To this day, I thank my father for teaching me all that he knows. I wouldn't be the strong person I am today without his mentorship.

I remember it was the summer of 2002: Joe Martin Field. My siblings and I lived at the ballparks over the summer months. Most times, I would ask to be dropped off to watch games and eat the ballpark food. This summer stood out the most to me, and I still replay the events of a particular day often in my mind. My younger sister and I were horsing around. She was being her goofy self, making me laugh at the simplest things and poking fun at our younger brother who was playing ball. She decided to coax me into walking around the ballpark. I picked up what she was putting down. She had crush on a boy in her middle school who was playing catch with another boy on the other side of the bench of the opposing team. She started to get shy as we walked towards them.

I can't recall my children's first words, or how old I was when I got my period. I do, however, remember how warm the sun was that day and how bright the light was that shone around his image. His curly hair poked out from underneath his red ball hat, and his bright blue eyes radiated in excitement. I couldn't stop staring, and to my disbelief, I realized he was staring right back at me. That moment felt like a lifetime, but it passed in seconds; suddenly we were smiling at each other. I heard a small whisper of what felt like wind: "*Him.*"

It was unlike anything I had ever encountered, and I felt this silly girl giggle come up. My heart was racing and pounding so hard against my chest. I felt butterflies in my stomach. Weeks went by and I couldn't get his face out of my head. I blamed my hormones: schoolgirl crush. I honestly didn't know what to think about it. I didn't have any girlfriends. I couldn't relate to, or trust, any girls I knew. My guy friends were pigs. How could a fifteen-year-old, dare I say it, fall in love? I was so young and immature; I didn't even know his name. Nothing made sense. I decided this was just foolishness and tried to ignore my feelings. I had never seen him before. I had never played ball with or against him. I asked my sister if she recalled his face from her school. She didn't. He remained a mystery. I gave up and assumed he was a city boy. I'd probably never see him again. End of story.

Fast forward to the fall of that same year. I had just had my birthday, and I was now in grade eleven. On the third day of school, I was walking the hallways in between classes when I saw that same red hat leaning against a locker. Other students were crowding around him. As I approached, he slowly started to turn in my direction. I looked away. I didn't want him knowing I already saw him. *Him!* I couldn't stop myself, the sides of my mouth started to jerk upwards all on their own. I remember thinking, "Am I smirking?" I tried to look forward, but his bright blue eyes were on me again.

His mouth opened wide, and I heard the words "No fucking way!" as I strode by. I giggled out loud. Something inside me compelled me to look back. It was the best decision I have ever made. I caught everything: his attention, awareness, surprise, and happiness in that moment.

I couldn't pay attention to anything after that. I kept questioning what I saw, what I was feeling. I daydreamed that he actually liked looking at me. Honestly, I was nothing special. I kept to myself, looked down often, couldn't relate to other girls, and stayed inside a classroom during lunch period. My makeup was all over the place, my clothes were second hand, I was built like a little boy, and I loved baseball. I was simple and plain. I was in a state of shock at the idea of him talking to me. What if he did? What would I say? How would I say anything to him without looking like a big dork?

The end of the day came so slowly. My emotions were all over the place. My locker was in the worst part of school: the Common Room, where all the rich, preppy wannabes sat, judging everyone from the sidelines. Ever seen the movie *Mean Girls*? Seriously, it was exactly like that bullshit!

My locker was beside a girl who kept her dramatic life on her locker shelf for everyone to see. She seemed to have a different boyfriend every month. I did, however, get a kick out of her. She was by far the most entertaining girl I befriended during my high school years. I was listening to her talk about her latest romantic drama that day, when suddenly she stopped mid-sentence and gave me a look. Then she tilted her eyes to look behind me. I knew immediately what that meant: *he* was approaching. Dear God, please no!

How did he find me? Fuck. Ass. Shit. Fuck! I froze completely. No joke, I buried my head in my locker. Suddenly, he was right beside me, and I could feel his breath—it had a sweet but spicy, earthy smell. I felt my whole face go from warm to hot.

"Hi. My name is Brad."

I still couldn't move; I was shaking. I felt like everybody was watching me and thinking what an idiot I was. I thought, "Now everyone here will most definitely know I am a virgin. Fuck. So will he! Say something!"

"Elisha, you're being rude," said my locker neighbour. "Her name is Elisha."

Thanks, girl next door.

I don't know how things are done now, but when I was in school, first you got someone's phone number. Then you asked them to go out. After that, it was holding hands during school while walking the hallways. At that point, you were a couple. He asked for my number; he had to write it down. I was still shaking—blushing in shock.

Later, he would often make fun of me for blushing. I would never admit to it. He loved teasing me, holding me in his arms, and calling me cute. He knew I hated being called cute. He also knew he was the only man allowed to call me cute and the first to make blush.

For weeks he would call. We talked for hours. In school we kept to ourselves. I didn't like being a spectacle, but I liked the idea of courting. We bypassed the high school couple rules. He learned about my family's values and that my father was my best friend, an honest man in everything he did—a God-fearing man. During one phone call I remember hearing his mother call him Bradley. I refused to call him anything else after that. He was Bradley—my Bradley.

I wasn't really allowed to date, but I shared with my father what Bradley had come to mean to me in such a short amount of time. My father, who has my greatest respect, trusted me then as he does now. He wasn't worried, and I always took this as his blessing. Our first date was walking to the Burger Bar on our lunch break. Bradley offered to buy a milkshake. I giggled when he suggested we share. I knew he only had enough money for one. I panicked when he politely asked me what flavour I wanted. I couldn't understand how there could be so many damned flavours of ice cream. Fucking banana?! Are you kidding me? Who would order that shit? I tried to put it back on him to make the decision, but he insisted it was a treat for me, and I started to feel guilty.

My inner voice came into play. "Be honest," it said. I looked into his eyes, struck by what I had never noticed before: in his left eye he had a ring of brown encircling his blue eye. My first thought was how beautiful, and how rare. But then I remembered what happened to people who were different in *The Chrysalids*, a novel by John Wyndham I had just finished reading. In that reality, even the slightest deformity would render a person a mutant to be discarded. I laughed out loud at the thought, and he gave me an odd look. I quickly recovered and bluntly requested a vanilla shake, saying that is how ice cream should be. His smile grew instantly.

"Funny—that is the only kind I like as well," he said.

As we walked back towards school, I gave him a hard time about liking vanilla shakes. I assumed he was like every other guy who agreed with a girl just to make her happy and, in some cases, keep the peace. He teased me back, pointing out that it was the gentlemanly thing to do.

That evening on our phone date, he asked me why I was laughing before I ordered the vanilla milkshake. I tried to deflect the question, saying I didn't know what he was talking about. He gave me a choice to share it over the phone or suffer the consequences of a public interrogation at school the next day.

Bradley was never to be underestimated. He was the most persistent pain-in-the-ass man I have ever had to deal with. He wouldn't let you off the hook—*ever!* Especially if you got caught in a lie or dancing around the truth. He would eventually get it out of you. I have never seen anyone so determined. So, I confessed the truth over the phone. I did not want to blush in front of him or look into his eyes. I was a coward. I told him that I loved the ring of brown in his left eye but that if he'd been a character in *The Chrysalids*, he'd have been called a mutant and thrown away. I will never forget how loudly he laughed at me. I started to laugh too, and I realized that he didn't mind me teasing him back. I high fived myself in the air, ecstatic at the idea that I could be funny too.

Elisha: 1; Bradley: 0.

Then his sly, sharp, ever-so-quiet voice said, "Well, I guess you don't want to kiss a mutant now, do you?"

Elisha: 1; Bradley: 1.

I had never kissed a boy. Not like this. Not like Bradley. In the movie *Hitch*, it's explained that men should lean in ninety percent and women, ten percent. That was how he lured me in. Most times I didn't see it coming. My cheek would be turned the other way and just as I turned my head, my lips would meet his. Surprise! Bradley always played games. He often used his humour in a playful and cheeky way.

We had been seeing each other for just about two months and were growing quite close. One Friday evening the phone rang. It was super late. In our house anything past 7:00 p.m. was late. I remember this call being well past 9:00 p.m. My father answered. He was not impressed. I heard Bradley's voice on the other end and loud music in the background.

"Turn the music down!" he barked. Then to me he said, "Hey. Come to my party."

I noticed something was different in his voice. He didn't sound like himself. I found it super rude and annoying: the people in the background, the loud music, and the constant interruption. There was no room for conversation—not like the ones we usually shared together. He was really talking *a lot*.

"Kempster's Garage Party, baby!" he yelled.

I thought to myself, "Now he is talking about himself in the third person?" I was so confused; was he talking to me? I overheard a girl talking on the other end of the phone. "Holy fuck. That's just wonderful," I thought to myself. She was loud and repeating herself to him. She wanted to know who he was talking to.

"My girlfriend!" he answered her.

The girl asked why I wasn't there. I asked Bradley who she was, and he told me her name. This chick was the slut bag of high school. That sounds awful, but she loved the title. She made it known that she lost her virginity while drunk at a party. I had no patience nor room in my life for girls like that, although I realized most girls who acted that way had low self-esteem—no love for themselves or their bodies. Guys fed on that like fucking sharks.

I never understood that. Why do so many people in today's world ask for others to have relationships with them when they don't have a relationship with themselves? If you want to be respected and valued, stop acting cheap! I told Bradley I wasn't interested. "Have a good night. I'll see you at school," I said and hung up the phone.

After that night something in Bradley changed. He was constantly tired in school. He only came to my locker out of obligation. His energy completely shifted. The phone calls stopped. Just like that, I was a ghost. Within a couple of weeks, he had another girl on his arm. I was broken-hearted. I felt rejected and wanted to know why or what I had done to lose him. I was two grades older, and my development level was most definitely higher. I blamed his immaturity.

Then why, I would ask myself, did this hurt so much? He didn't want our relationship anymore, but I didn't know why. I had no peace, but I masked my heartache and carried on. Time would eventually tell the truth—it always does! Fifteen years later, I overheard a conversation between my son Tanner and Bradley. Tanner, my beautiful and very protective son, asked Bradley, "Was my mother not good enough for you in high school?" Talk about being put on the spot. Bradley giggled—a soft, deep, and smooth sound ruffling in his throat.

"Tanner, the truth is *I* wasn't good enough for your mother. I thought she was better off without me. I hurt your mom by telling my guy friends my reason for dumping her was that she was a square. She wasn't cool enough for me. She wouldn't drink, smoke, flirt, or have sex with me. Your mom, well, she was built like a Corvette, and I was more like an old Buick."

I watched my son's eyes tear up as these words poured out of Bradley. To my surprise he replied, "You said my mom was built like a Corvette in high school. What is she now?"

Of course, that was all he heard. I laughed to myself that he was a mini-Bradley in the making. Bradley looked directly at me as I entered the room. "She's *my* Corvette."

It took me by surprise. I'd been expecting a punchline. I figured he'd either come up with something to tease me about and then call me "my love" to suck up to me. Or he'd call me "Linda"—the nickname he insisted on using for me. It was his way to point out how overwhelming my presence could be— running a million miles a minute and not taking a breath or slowing down for a single moment. "Linda, *listen* to me!" Bradley would laugh.

"Why are you calling me that?" I asked once, annoyed and confused. He never gave me a straightforward answer, but somehow it stuck. People still call me Linda to this day, and now I get a sense of comfort from it. My daughter and son use it often to put me in my place when I am acting over the top and driving them crazy. A girlfriend, when she sees me stressed out and constantly repeating myself, whispers in my ear, "You're being a Linda." I hear it most often when I break down and cry in defeat, heartache, and pain.

Linda: 1; Bradley: 2.

My love, may our light and love
together shine and transform all darkness and fear.
All my love, Bradley

(From Bradley's birthday card to me, September 2019)

TWO

I graduated high school in 2004. I had a kid in 2007, got married in 2009, and had another kid in 2011. By 2013, I was divorced. In 2012, as my marriage was ending, I moved to Kamloops, BC to go to school for Cosmetology.

I left my children with their father in Prince Rupert, BC. Yes, I left my kids. I can give you plenty of excuses: I needed to build a career to support them; my schooling was too far away. The truth is, I could have gone to Cosmetology school in Prince George, which is closer, and lived with my parents. But I was tired—tired of being a mom, of being a wife, and of having to set my life aside. So, I left. I lived my way—free of all obligations. I ran. I played the victim and took no responsibility. I blamed everything and everyone to justify my selfishness. I ran away like a coward and abandoned those kids; at the time, my son was five and my daughter, two.

I boarded with my aunt while I attended school in Kamloops. There, I was able to be what I wanted people to see me as: single, strong, and sexy as hell. It felt like a whole other life. I loved that no one knew me, and I could decide who the new me would be—

especially coming from a small town like Prince Rupert, where everybody knew who you were and what you ate for breakfast. I couldn't stand the attention. I couldn't breathe.

Pain changes a person. In the last few years before I left Prince Rupert, I had kept busy to numb my pain—pain from babies, from an unhappy marriage, and from toxic relationships. I was broken, but instead of taking time to heal, I pushed on and forward. I wasn't the soft spoken, honest, and kind person I had been in high school any longer. I had given everything I had for years, and I wanted to take something back—no matter the cost.

School didn't start until September, and I made sure to get to Kamloops by the end of August to find a job. I applied everywhere for serving positions. Every place said the same thing: "You're two weeks late. We already did our hiring." The one place I really didn't want to apply to was a stripper bar and night club. But I really needed a job and, unfortunately, they were the only place that called me back. They offered me four days a week part time.

"Great! What will family back home think?" I thought to myself.

My first shift was a Saturday night. I will never forget what my new boss said to me as I opened her office door. "Oh! You actually showed up."

"Dear God," I thought to myself. "Is it really that bad?"

She must have seen the look of surprise on my face. "Usually when I tell new hires they have to wear lingerie on Wednesdays, I never see their faces again," she laughed. I followed her to the POS system where servers rang in their drink orders. I saw pool tables to my right, just before the front entrance, and took note of the two bouncers. I also saw two men enter at the same time. One was pale and dark, with a shaved head. The other had longer curly hair, a tall, strong build—*holy fuck!* It was Bradley!

I was trying to keep my attention on my new boss's instructions. She had to ask me if I was ok a few times. My heart was halfway out of my chest. I couldn't wrap my mind around the fact he was *here*—of all places! It was my first night at a new job. I had just moved here for this school, and *there he is!* My dreamboat guy. The one that got away. Dig me dead and bury me pregnant!

I avoided going close for most of my shift. I kept doubting if it was really Bradley. I hadn't seen him in ten years. Finally, I saw his drink was empty and so was his friend's; I grabbed some balls and walked over. On the way over, I realized how much I had changed, in my appearance alone. I wasn't this innocent Virgin Mary anymore. I was stunning, experienced, and renewed, or at least I looked like it. The soft, long, dirty brown hair and plain skin had changed to purple hair, makeup, and tattoos.

As I got closer, a series of thoughts ran through my head: he won't recognize me; I am the one who feels she missed out; he probably doesn't even recall my name; he was the player in high school.

Too late. I was right in front of them both. Without either of them taking a glance up at me, I asked for their order. "Can I get either of you a refill?"

Bradley, with his head still down, responded, "No thanks."

"Are you sure about that, Kempster?"

I had often called him Kempster on the baseball field when we were young. Sometimes I used it when I was mad and trying to be serious enough to grab his attention. When I used it this time, his eyes looked up in complete disbelief. The same words came out as when he saw me in high school for the first time. "No fucking way."

There it was: the same mutant eye, same eye contact, same expression. It was my Bradley. I went about my work, but he kept staring intently at me from the other end of the bar and shaking his head. I guess he was in shock. I was just happy that, after all these years, I had finally got his attention.

We stalked one another online for weeks and Facebook said it all. He had a girlfriend, the same one from high school. I was surprised to see him with the same woman after all these years, especially knowing about his many indiscretions in the past. I wanted to appear single and unattached from any obligations. I tried to keep my past life a secret—my kids, my failed marriage—but, of course, he saw what I tried so hard to conceal.

For years, Bradley and I argued over who saw who first that day. I always knew it was me, but he wouldn't confess the truth until, in a Valentine's Day card years later, he wrote:

> You're right. I didn't see you first in Kamloops. My heart leapt when I heard your voice call me Kempster. I will never forget that rush I felt. After all that time and change, I was still Kempster.
>
> All my love Hunny,
> Bradley.
> February 2019

Linda: 2; Bradley: 2.

I would be lying if I said I didn't see past Bradley's mask when I ran into him after all those years. His actions spoke louder than words in Kamloops. He was lost and defeated because of his life-style, work environment, and the people he chose to be around. I saw myself in him. I was in a lot of pain as well, and two wounded people got together in their time of brokenness. I believe we felt safety and a sense of relief in one another. What better distraction than hooking up with someone who was in the same boat?

It wasn't much of a relationship, but Bradley and I put up with one another. We didn't have a right to say a lot to each other about our histories and our bad habits. I certainly didn't speak up—I didn't care enough. Our time together was very limited. We only got together to take from each other. It was a false sense of fulfillment—an attachment. Most of the time we were together, I was just company for Bradley while he was high. He didn't like being alone when doing drugs like MDMA or cocaine. I only showed up in hopes of getting some dick. He knew this and used it as a manipulation tactic to serve his purposes as well. For some strange reason, we were constantly drawn to one another. We were both operating on the same frequency of low vibrational energies. There was no judgement, therefore we could stand one another's chaotic lifestyles.

I was disappointed in myself and this man, who I had fantasized about since I was a young girl. My first thought: *this* was the boy I saw on the baseball field that magical day? He had he become *this* man? My second: he was a loser. My third: we were both losers. My selfishness clouded my sense of worth and values. All I had ever wanted was him. While we were together in Kamloops, I took what I wanted from him: sex, period. The rest of it? Not my business, nor my problem. I witnessed Bradley do everything: drinking, drugs, and sex. I stood back, and by doing so, I encouraged his behaviour. I was very unhealthy myself and supported his addictions. We were both broken and due to that state of brokenness, all we left were trails of pain—hurting others but mostly hurting ourselves.

Bradley was notorious for falling asleep with food in his hands. The smell of stale food, sweat, and piss was the scene I walked into many times. I would place him in the shower and look after his puppy who usually smelled of shit. So many times, I would just come to clean, stock his fridge, tuck him into bed, and take care of his dog, who needed to be walked and played with. Watching Bradley attempt to stay sober so he could earn an income was like watching a horror movie. He was charged twice with DUI and lost his driver's licence. I became his chauffeur, driving him to and from work. We were always stopping by the liquor store. He would be so irritable until a cold drink would touch his hands and lips. Then he would be excited to be in my company. I would be lying if I didn't admit I preferred this Bradley. He was funny, flirty, energetic, and, in a way, made you his whole world. He would take me out to eat and make me feel special. All because that drink would make him comfortable enough to express who he wanted to be all along. I liked that he wanted me around. I liked being needed again—and he did need me. He needed my help.

Eventually, reality slapped me in the face. It was July 2013. School was finished, and I was moving back to Prince George. At the age of thirty, divorced, and with two kids, I was moving back in with my parents and starting a new career. Bradley and I ended our fling and lost contact. Shortly after I returned to Prince George, I found out that Bradley was with another woman and had gotten her pregnant. Although they decided to abort the pregnancy, he wanted to make it work with her and give their relationship a chance. I remember hearing this and being so grateful I had escaped. I felt as if I was being given a second chance to make things right with my own life and path. I buckled down and was determined to regain what I had lost.

At the same time though, I felt hurt by this news. After all I had done for him, I hoped at least I had left an impression and that all my good deeds during our time together in Kamloops had meant something. Although I was relieved I wasn't with Bradley anymore, I couldn't help but feel that I had been rejected by yet another man. But I carried on with my life, and so did he. I had made a fantasy a reality, and the experience had been disappointing.

My new career was demanding and drained me of all my energy. I was a single mother of two kids who hadn't seen me in a year. They didn't know me, nor I them. We were all living with my parents, and while I was trying to rebuild my life, it seemed impossible. For some reason, I kept replaying my time in Kamloops in my head. I remembered how free I felt, but also how lost I was. I realized how unhappy I truly was. I often wondered about Bradley and dwelled on the pain of losing someone who seemed as lost as me. So, I did what I do best and distracted myself with another man to escape the pain. I lied to myself that this would make me happy. I was too chicken shit to drink or do drugs, so men were my addiction. Once again, I took from someone else. I was hurting and, due to this, I hurt other people. I just tried to fake my way through the reality of my lost life.

One afternoon in November, my sister called to inform me that a Bradley Kempster had been harassing her about my whereabouts. He wanted to get in touch with me. At the first opportune moment, I gave him a ring. I found out he was living with his mother. We both were in the same town again. Once again, two unhealthy people decided to distract one another from each other's pain.

This time, we chose to make a go of a life together. We bought a house, I had a small business going at that point, and Bradley worked as a track press operator. We were a family—Bradley, me, my two children, and *three dogs*. The dogs were something Bradley demanded for his happiness. Trust me, it took years to convince him to come down to three from the five he originally wanted. We had Ayms, Astin, and Altas, three purebred Shetland sheepdogs. Ayms was with Bradley when I met him in Kamloops, trained and well kept. By the time we got our girl Astin, a year after purchasing our house, everything went sideways. She was beautiful but her high anxiety and need for attention drained the family. She drove me crazy. She wasn't a good fit for our small home or our busy family and did not take well to living with another dog. I tried to convince Bradley that Astin would be happier in a home where she was the only dog, but he refused to acknowledge her needs. He wanted his dream of owning several shelties and creating his fantasy family of fur babies. Out of spite, and an act of selfishness, Altas came into the picture. We had no business owning three dogs. We could barely afford the needs of two. Altas was a thoughtless purchase—a desperate grasp at happiness and, I believe, an attempt to fill a void for Bradley. We couldn't keep up with these three dogs, and in the end, they suffered from our neglect. They were never disciplined, and eventually all became crazy and annoying creatures—they were like wild animals.

I honestly thought if we gave each other everything we wanted, we would be happy. That was a mistake. There was always one thing holding us back from a happy life. It was a distraction that Bradley couldn't control, and it always came first. Our life, growth, and love were drowning in last place. I knew about his secret, but I still hoped that if I gave him a home, children, dogs, and me as his wife, he would leave behind that one thing holding him hostage. That one thing stopped him from truly living in peace. I soon came to realize he was incapable of escaping this habit. And that's because it wasn't a habit. It was an illness—a disease that consumed all of him.

I am blessed to have a friend and a lover like you in my life.
You have cared for me and loved me despite all my flaws
and mistakes. For this I hope you will never leave my side.
All my love, Bradley

(From Bradley's Christmas card to me, December 2015)

THREE

Bradley was a force to be reckoned with. He was an intelligent man with a background in psychology. I loved his way with words. I was amazed by his ability to explain complicated matters in the simplest and most beautiful way. Bradley had the kindest voice I have ever heard, especially when he was speaking on behalf of others. He could raise others up to be the best versions of themselves.

But, if I am completely blunt and honest, he could also be a manipulative, arrogant asshole. When Bradley didn't get his way, his anger and cruelty came into play. I witnessed over the years the fear Bradley instilled in many; most were family and people who loved him. I bore the worst of his behaviour as my fear of him was the greatest. He knew this well and took advantage of my vulnerability often. He was my weakness.

I didn't mind the asshole part at all—shit, we all have our moments. I would often say to him, "You're allowed to be an asshole; just remember to be my asshole." Him being an asshole was one thing, but when he drank, his behaviour was unendurable. What made everything intolerable was the fact that Bradley's illness had warped his thinking, putting him in a state of denial.

The truth is Bradley was an alcoholic.

You can look up the definition of alcoholism, but I think the following metaphor describes Bradley's behaviour better. He was like the character Smeagol from *The Lord of the Rings*. Smeagol is a sweet and kind hobbit who goes fishing and berry picking with his friend, until he comes across this ring with terrible powers, and he transforms into the evil, possessive, corrupt Gollum. In the novel, Gollum often refers to this ring as "my precious." As long as that ring is in his hands, Gollum is in control and the vibrant, warm, and healthy-looking Smeagol is nowhere to be found. Gollum kills for this ring and lives a life of solitude—away from life, love, light, and happiness.

I started to understand how sick Bradley was. How did I know? The abuse. When Bradley was drunk, the verbal abuse would strangle the life right out of me. He would call me a bitch, a selfish whore, and a terrible useless mother. Psychological abuse came in the form of gaslighting and manipulation. I kept trying to tell him he had a problem, but he would turn it around on me, blaming me for why he drank. I didn't know who or what I was, and I started to second guess my innocence as well as my identity as a woman and a mother. Most heartbreaking was the sexual abuse I was subjected to. It's hard for me to write about, but when he was drunk, he would torture me, make me feel ashamed, and take away parts of me that left me feeling exposed—constantly exposed, vulnerable, and in a state of fear.

I was terrified of him.

When I would try to help, I would be punished. It was Gollum at his finest. No matter what I did, nothing worked. I would try to control the amount Bradley would drink per day. I would place boundaries and limit certain liquors. It got to a point where

I would buy his beer just to set financial limits. I even drank with him to try to set a standard. Honestly, you name it, I tried every fucking thing possible. Nothing worked. After all my attempts, I would curl up into a ball and crash. I was spent—physically, mentally, and emotionally. Gollum would drain every ounce of energy I had left. The manipulation and gaslighting got so bad, I started to question my own sanity and reality. When this was happening, Bradley would use any excuse to make me the problem. Anytime I mentioned his drinking, Gollum's wrath was unleashed. The fighting would get so bad I had to ask him to leave. He would take off and stay in a hotel. He'd disappear for days without me knowing where he was. Our home turned into a war zone, and our kids were subjected to it. We separated three times. After the second separation, I remember he said to me, "If I ever leave again, I'm never coming back." This was what I feared most and due to this I put up with the abuse for longer than I should have.

What do most people do to save something that isn't worth saving? They put a bandage over the problem and try to disguise it as happiness. In August 2019, Bradley proposed in Victoria at Butchart Gardens. I will never forget how I felt and the words that came out of his mouth:

Elisha, I love you and want to spend the rest of my life with you. I will protect you, provide for you, and together, we will build our empire. You are everything to me and I will spend the rest of my existence by your side, in sickness and in health. Will you marry me?

To this day I remember how my body felt and the thoughts that ran through my mind. My body was vibrating—shaking from the inside out. I felt ashamed. How long had I waited to see this man down on one knee? To hear these words come from his lips? In that moment, which I replay often in my mind today, I saw how blind and selfish I was. How could I ask a sick man to give more? All that he said to me, down on one knee, was a lie. He loved me and wanted a life together? He wanted to protect and to provide? Bradley did none of these things for himself—not a single one. How could he do them for someone else?

I said yes, but with all my heart, I was screaming *no!* Before me was a man who I knew couldn't take care of himself; his family had been suffering from the fact for years. I couldn't sleep after the proposal, knowing full well what needed to happen next. Weeks went by, and his drinking got worse. He started using drugs again because alcohol wasn't enough to numb his pain. I was terrified to confront him.

In September 2019, I handed back my engagement ring. This separation was by far the ugliest. For the first time ever, I mentioned the words "drinking problem" and "alcoholic" in the same sentence. Bradley went mad. At one point in *The Lord of the Rings*, Gollum bites off his friend Frodo's finger to keep the ring. Bradley bit his way through everything that mattered most to us. He threatened our home, took away everything the kids cared about, racked up thirty thousand dollars of debt in one month, and the one that stabbed me deeply? The thing he knew would kill a part of my heart? It was my second biggest fear: he had an affair with another woman.

I have never crashed so hard in my life over so much pain. As I write these words now, I replay how broken I was—torn and shaken. Was I really such an awful woman to him? I still ask myself this question to this day as I try to make sense of what happened. Even now, tears swell in my eyes. I remember like it was yesterday—lying on the bathroom floor, making sounds I never thought possible. I wailed in agony with my eyes shut tight and my nose fully stuffed. I was barely able to catch my breath. My head was pounding from a migraine. I stayed on that cold, hard bathroom floor for a long time. My clothes were soaked in my tears, snot, and vomit.

Something inside me said, "You don't have to do this; you can end the pain by ending your life." For a moment, I went down that path. I really believed I couldn't bear it any longer. I was too chicken shit to start drinking. I was too much of a daddy's girl to get high on drugs—I still feared losing my father's respect. I honestly didn't want to numb myself anyway. Why not end the misery, by simply ending my life? Problem solved—no more pain and no more heartache.

But there was one thing that pulled me away from that thought. One thing that picked me up from the floor. *One*. It wasn't my kids or picturing my future and being happy again. It was the truth. It was the truth in my faith. Truth in my life has a name: Jesus.

Don't worry. I am not going to babble and preach to you. I really just want you, the reader, to know my faith saved my life that day. I am by far His biggest fan and owe Him everything. There was a beam of light that came through the bathroom window—a warmth I haven't ever felt before. It was a soothing comfort when I heard the message, but it didn't come in the form of words. It was more like a life-altering feeling down to my soul: "Everything is going to be ok!" Holding my head up for the first time in years, I did something I'd forgotten how to do—*breathe*. I took the biggest, deepest, and longest breath of my life and said these words: "Time to wake *up*, my love!" From that moment on,

I was never the same. I changed my whole being. I started to live my life openly, willingly, and took the pain. I would rather be in pain, than bear witness to it.

Linda: 3; Bradley: 2.

Trust when I say, love, that I want this as well and that
I will get there.
Be patient with me and momentous change will continue.
All my love, Bradley

(From Bradley's Valentine's Day card to me, February 2018)

FOUR

I was given a word for 2019. I kept hearing it on repeat everywhere I went: *perseverance*. It was easy enough to google the definition, but I wasn't meant to follow a script. I knew I needed to find my own meaning, something that resonated with me.

Bradley was gone, and I didn't know where he was or if he was safe. I was alone and hurting. I could barely think. I wouldn't go to work. I wouldn't eat. I was always tired. I could not function mentally or emotionally. I never wanted to leave my house.

My mother came by one afternoon after picking up the kids from school. She brought me into the bathroom and drew me a bubble bath. After helping me get into the hot tub, she looked at my worn, wet, and puffy eyes and caught my gaze with her bright blue eyes. "You are grieving him, the loss of him." She said it so softly and with all the love in her heart for me. Only a mother truly knows her daughter's heart as if it is her own.

She was right. At that point, I had been grieving the loss of this man for years. Our relationship was being destroyed by this disease. All that we built together was based on a lie. This wasn't true love, not with an illness controlling this man and all that he is. The disease was abusing and hurting him. In turn, he was hurting and abusing me. As they say, hurt people hurt people. I came to understand these words very well. I had allowed his illness to take over my life. It was a sickness that left me stranded and depressed. It resulted in an anger that drove me mad.

I realized that I had allowed the abuse because I did not truly love myself enough to put a stop to it. At the same time, I see now that my suffering allowed me to develop my ability to persevere and helped to define my character. Perseverance gave me hope for the first time ever. It prevented me from feeling disheartened when fear and doubt would attack me. It helped me see that I was worthy of love, and it was time to truly fall in love with me. That, to me, is perseverance.

Within two months of Bradley's departure, I started to rehabilitate my identity. I had been trapped for far too long in this sickness—this disease that had taken hold of my life. Everything from my home to my money and my mental stability had been robbed from me for years. It was time I stood up to it.

The very first thing I did was get my finances in order. Being financially secure felt like an enormous burden had finally been lifted. I could pay my bills, take care of the kids' extra needs, and still have money left over in my accounts. And the best part? No debt. I was restored knowing my money was in order and safe. I buckled down and worked harder than ever in my small but growing business. I made sure to only work part-time when my children were with me. When the children were with their father for his week, I would restore myself with personal time.

I prepared healthy meals and dove into meditation. Yoga became my sanctuary and safe haven. I rekindled friendships that had been lost or broken. For once, I actually had girlfriends that I would invite into my home. I cooked and entertained. I made amends with family I'd pushed away for years. In my spare time, I would read, pray, and be present. My eyes were open, my ears sharp, and my thinking changed—all because I opened my heart to be loved. By accepting this love, I knew how it felt to be truly in love. I saw myself transform, and I was in love with who I was becoming. A new experience for me took place. I had a relationship with myself. Before you ask anyone to come into your life and build a relationship with you, you must ask it of yourself.

I will never forget the one time ever I said the word "no" to the man I loved dearly but also feared. While I was in recovery and moving forward, Bradley never stopped the manipulation. I had to build a high-rise of boundaries. At times, they were only partly successful. He would, at random, show up at the kids' sports events, which made things even harder; it was very inappropriate. I would be at home building them up with love, courage, and strength. They would see my tears of forgiveness but still see my anguish. They didn't know or understand the full truth and why I kept them away from Gollum. He was convinced he had a right to be in their lives but made no attempt to see the damage he was causing. Empty promises were made and lies were told and, well, Momma Bear came out. I got angry.

I hadn't spoken to Bradley in three months at this point, but I knew I had to in order to protect the ones I love. I had a clear conversation with him; a line was drawn, and I put him in his place. I replay our meeting often in my head. Bradley was clever and the disease in this moment made him sadistic. He was hurting the children to get to me. At the same time, he wanted to keep me at arm's length. He didn't want to change and all of a sudden be around for the family. He wanted to maintain a lifestyle that I would no longer support or partake in and still hold on to us by attaching himself to the children.

He was crashing and getting a lot worse. On the outside, he looked ok. He had bought new clothes, was cleanshaven, and was spending money like water on his new woman. On the inside though, he was so lost. I saw through it all, using wisdom and truth. Wisdom is the perfect balance of intelligence and love. Without intelligence, you're ignorant. Without love you're arrogant. I wanted to tell him, "You can suck it, Bradley!"

Linda: 4; Bradley: 2.

Gollum began his attacks. He hunted his way through anything and would stop at nothing to get what he thought he deserved. When no one reacted the way he wanted, he became more lost and alone. I wouldn't give him an inch. I stood back and loved him but walked away from him and the disease. In February 2020, Bradley crashed completely. Five months after he separated from me and the children, he had lost everything—his job, his home, his health, and his mental stability. COVID-19, and all the chaos it brought, was on the horizon. Bradley had no choice but to attempt sobriety.

One early evening around that time, I saw his name on my phone. I had blocked his number, but I just happened to look at my phone at the exact time he called. Apparently, if you block a number, that person's name will still show up once on your phone when they try to call you. I saw his name flash briefly on my phone, and something in my heart told me I had to call him back. I really didn't want to. My mind raced. I didn't trust him, and I knew this was just another crash and that, in a couple of months, we'd go through the awful cycle again. I had been doing this for years. He was going to destroy my peace and all that I had built. I couldn't get involved.

What I knew in my head and what I felt in my heart were two very different things. I decided to bow my head to my heart and reached for a form of love: compassion. In my head, I heard my word for 2020, soft as a whisper: *truth*. I wanted to come to the truth in all this. We are all ordinary people but even so, we can, within ourselves, turn on a small light in a dark room. I did what I had to do because it was the right thing to do. I was responsible for bringing this man home and showing him the light.

In fact, I was commanded to.

A wonderful year my love; through our highs and through our lows we stuck together. I know we will never forget it, and never forget how strong we are and will be together.
All my love, Bradley

(From Bradley's Christmas card to me, December 2020)

FIVE

"Time to wake up, my love," Bradley whispered softly in my ear. I felt him running his cold hand in my hairline and across my cheekbone; he leaned in slightly to kiss my neck and lips until I fluttered my eyes open. I drifted back to sleep, but the smell of coffee woke me again. I found him sitting in his recliner, Bible in hand. He gave me his eyes—his bright blue and alive eyes. He motioned for me to come sit in his lap and drink the tea he had made for me. Together we sat. Together we read. Together we prayed. Together.

Bradley was healing. He was seeing the good in himself and forgiving the bad. By his side, I gave him love and compassion to raise him up as high as possible, to show him he was worthy—worthy as a husband, a father, a best friend, and a man. His heart had softened. I guided him to start loving himself, and to accept that love. Most importantly, Bradley started journaling again.

March 2020

I am grateful for the support of my family, for Elisha's love, and our journey together. I feel secure knowing that no matter what, there is someone to lean on in my difficult times. None of this was possible without Jesus. My Father led me through all these times. I learned what surrender feels like, how to rejoice in all things that are happening for me, and who to look to when fear attacks me. Elisha led me back. His love in her shines brightly. I was driving my life to ruins again from desires of the flesh and you brought Elisha back to me again. You sent me your angel. She is my angel. Father, you are shining through her. Thank you, Father. I am so blessed.

It had been six months since Bradley had a drink, six months since I received that phone call from a broken, scared, and lonely man. As a result of his pain, he had lost sight of his purpose. He faced his pain and with my love and help, we became one. One soul united together in all things. Everything was beginning to be restored. All the intimacies were aligning: financial, intellectual, physical, recreational, emotional, and spiritual. I was starting to breathe again. Slowly. I still had pain that remained due to broken trust. The difference was Bradley, for the first time ever, sat across from me. He stayed as I broke down in tears over the pain he caused us. I wasn't lying alone on the bathroom floor anymore. He was right there, taking in all the sounds, bearing my anxiety, and never once leaving my side. At times, I would get triggered and just start crying. In silence and in love, he would care for me. Sometimes, when he felt helpless and lost knowing he created this pain inside me and was unable to fix it, he would simply ask, "Is there anything I can do for you, my love?" Most times I would disappear in a hot bath with a lot of bubbles, peppermint tea in hand. I would sing as loudly as I could as singing always soothed me. Other times I needed to be held; I would sit in his lap, face tucked in his neck, tears and snot streaming down my face and all over his shirt.

He was my best friend and the strongest man I knew. He held me so close—into his very being. We breathed together. It was perfect love driving out all fear. He taught me to centre my state of mind to stay present. Bradley had a book entitled *Peaceful Warrior*, and he often quoted three questions from it to settle me down. With his soft lips against my ear, he would whisper, "Where are you, my love?"

"I am here," I would reply.

"What time is it?" he would gently encourage.

"Now," I would whisper back to him.

"Who are you?" he would ask, his firm voice awakening me.

"This moment!" I would state back to him, becoming still in his arms.

Linda: 4; Bradley: 3.

To this day, I use his teachings often with the children. Most times my son grabs my eyes with his and repeats these same three questions to centre me. When I would enter a state of panic, Bradley would grab my face and connect our foreheads together. I would do the same for him. I would see his struggling mind and tired, sleepless eyes. It didn't matter where we were—in the kitchen, shower, anywhere—we would connect our foreheads and share the load. Together. Today, my daughter uses her little hands on my face to remind me of his touch and warmth. She does this often with me. She watched Bradley's every move with me.

Bradley could never apologize to me, but with his actions he did so much more. This created a change within the home among all of us. His presence was uplifting and challenged us to want to be more—more compassionate, patient, and filled with integrity. During all this, I was standing back, feeling so proud. He was driven in purpose by healing and softening his heart, knowing he was safe in my arms.

While Bradley could never say sorry to me, he did apologize to my son. He cried for what I believe was the first time ever in his life. I mean he really cried. I will never forget that day. He had held on to so much guilt about how he left the children during the last separation. He couldn't look my son in the eye. He knew my son and I were very close and that in Bradley's absence, a young boy took care of his mom. My little boy became a man overnight. They sat together at the kitchen table, and Bradley told him how sorry he was for all the pain he caused him. The pain was so deep that my son ran away in anger. He had told me before how cruel he thought Bradley was before he came back to us. Looking at me sitting alone, seeing my pain, he had asked, "Who is going to love you?" It was a sweet boy's question to a mother who he saw as his everything.

After watching this young boy run into his room in anger, Bradley looked down at his hands and broke down. He started to weep and make the same sounds I had made when he left us. I realized, in this moment, that Bradley had been the same hurt, lost, and angry little boy as my son except he had never received an apology from the people who had hurt him. And so, he remained a broken man.

Slowly, I carefully reached across the kitchen table and placed my hand on his forearm and said, "He loves you; give him time. Together we will get through this." I began to comfort him, and we cried together, head on top of head, the sounds of our tears overlapping one another. We both knew this was a deep, sharp pain inside of Bradley; a little boy was coming out to heal.

Without either of us realizing it, another one joined us. There was my son standing before Bradley, lips trembling, eyes red, and tears streaming down his face. Bradley looked up into his eyes as he stood before us. "I am sorry Dad for leaving in anger, but I needed a moment before telling you this: I forgive you and I love you." Bradley was never a stepfather to Tanner; he was his dad. In that moment, two little boys held one another and cried together.

Life was improving but Bradley still struggled. He was facing pain that had been stored inside since he was young. Often, we would talk about his deepest and most traumatizing memories. He was molested when he was eight years old by a family member. His father abandoned the family when Bradley was thirteen— and that was when Bradley started drinking. He had always looked up to his mother and had to witness her heartbreak from this event. He had been a talented pitcher, but an injury was mishandled by certain coaches Bradley had trusted. They covered up the pain in his arm and destroyed his future in baseball. He had been drugged and raped when he was twenty-two. After rejection and abuse by women he dated, he started dabbling in hard drugs in his early twenties. He got a woman pregnant, and she had an abortion. As his finances deteriorated, he turned to alcohol more and more often.

By his mid-twenties, he had nothing to live off or show for himself. He wrote his mother a letter expressing his state of mind and the circumstances he was in, begging to come home. The drugs stopped, but the drinking never did. He was an abusive alcoholic to me, the love of his life. He stole money and drowned our family in debt. He cheated on me multiple times during our separations and had an affair during the time we were engaged.

Bradley shoved all his pain way down deep inside him.

Drinking numbed the pain and helped him to cope. He just could not face his worth as a man. For years, I understood it was something more—drinking was always the mask. He was in so much pain and refused to forgive himself. He would always be the helper but could not accept help himself. He brought so much love and joy to others, but he remained an empty vessel. He was constantly over-compensating, especially as a father. Out of all his pain, there were three things he struggled with the most: his father's desertion when Bradley needed him the most; taking an innocent life through abortion; and the abuse and violence he inflicted on me. I forgave him but he said that didn't matter to him. In a journal entry, he stated what he believed his sole purpose and identity was.

March 2020

I have done many things and have often questioned my lack of contentment. I must confess that anything I do and or touch I master, and I get bored easily as it brings no challenge. I struggled to find and define my purpose as a man, until I became a father. I was meant to be a father. I am humbling myself and relinquishing control to understand fatherhood.

Bradley allowed me passage into his heart with open access to his pain, and I gently guided his journey towards healing. I saw him transform, his heart softening over the children. By accepting how I loved and treated him, he in turn did the same for the children.

I wrote him letters to remind him that he was beautiful as a man—not just as a husband or a father—but as a man first. He needed to be a man who he could identify with and love, unconditionally. I led the rehabilitation of someone who didn't deem himself worthy of love or forgiveness. He grew in wisdom and became something extraordinary: a free man. His eyes were bright and fixed on the horizon. His ears were ready for hearkening and recognition. His voice was full of drive and purpose. His head was lifted in courage, and his spirit was led by perfect love. He was beautiful. I would remind him that I dared not take the credit for this. I told him, "I am a leader, but I am not always in front. I do, however, know who I follow."

Bradley would hear me repeat these words every time he thanked me for saving him and giving him new direction. All I did was take his hand and guide him to the path that had been there all along. Something greater than me took over his heart and spirit: faith. Faith allowed him to believe in things he couldn't see and gave him hope that the future held a brighter path for him to follow. Faith took hold of Bradley and, with truth, guided his light. He felt it in everything he touched as a man, husband, and father. He found his true Father and allowed that love to be expressed in everything he did. Bradley was starting to forgive himself. He expressed this in his journal, but also, and more loudly than ever, in the letters he wrote to his son and daughter.

May 5, 2020
Come to me and I will listen and love you, always.

Tanner,
I love you, buddy. You're my best friend. I pray for you often. I want to remind you Tanner, that you are a very unique young man, so strong in your heart and worthy of love. I am proud that I have the privilege to call you

my son. Our Father in heaven has blessed me in more ways than I will ever be able to explain. It is because of His love, grace, and mercy that I am the man I am today. His faith in me never changed or left me empty. Even through difficult times, He kept me safe and watched over those I love. I hope that you will come to see that He is doing the same for you and will never stop. One day you will look back on your life and see how important your mistakes and failures are. One day you'll be able to see that sometimes your triumphs and celebrations only exist because of past errors. A mistake isn't really a mistake if you're meant to grow and learn from it. In those moments, take heart. You will grow stronger spiritually from the work of our Father. Then your life will be seen and understood. Everything happens for a reason, Son. It isn't our job to control everything, to worry about the past or fear the future, or to figure out why things happen. Our job is to love, to surrender, to obey, and to have faith that our Father knows what is best and will always keep us safe. He is our refuge and fortress.

All my love Tanner,
Dad.

May 5, 2020
I am always here if you need my heart or a hug.

Hailey,
I love you, little one. I missed you so much. I am so excited to hang out with you. I was thinking of you and remembered that Teddy and Bonka need fixing. I checked

them out and sewed them up. I also fixed the piggy suit that Gaffer loves so much! The doggies sure love you and Tanner. I missed your hugs and snuggles, but more than that, I missed all your questions. I love answering your questions.

I want to spend more time with you, Hunny. I have some ideas we could try. Is there anything you want to do with me? I think we will be able to try your telescope out. Or perhaps we could head out rock hunting too.

I am so proud to call you my daughter. You love so freely and feel so deeply. I know our Father in heaven has big plans for your future. You will be great and shine in everything you do.

All my love little one, my best friend,
Dad.

We had been together for almost a decade; in that time, Bradley was clean and sober for just six months. I would love to say that during those six months it was all sunshine and rainbows, but that would be far from the truth. He was irritable and tired all the time. One step in the wrong direction and he would lose it, which was not at all in his character—the man had more patience than me. The physical signs of withdrawal, like nausea and fatigue, appeared often. He was constantly restless and rarely slept.

The physical pain—where do I even begin to explain the physical pain? Bradley was slowly opening his heart to change and healing his deep wounds, turning them into scars. In time, love remained; however, the physical pain of his body would not let him rest. Years of neglect caught up with him and his body suffered greatly. I understood more than ever why Bradley drank. It wasn't just to numb his mind; he needed to numb the pain of his body. I am not a doctor, but I knew him best and saw his bad habits when it came to his physical health. I made sure to cook healthy meals for him every day and decreased his sugar intake to a bare minimum. He ate so much, more than I had ever seen him eat before. To me, it was very evident how malnourished he was. His body had been starving for years. The problem was his pain only increased. He was eating but he wasn't moving. Bradley easily started gaining weight and with no sleep and no energy, he just ballooned out. He had ignored his body by not limiting his drinking and stress. I believe this was part of the cause of his many health issues: abscesses, migraines, and hernias. Bradley also convinced himself that lymph nodes in his left leg were the issue. Deep down I knew there was more to it.

Several radiologists over many years told him the exact same answers. Ultrasounds, X-rays, and MRIs all showed the same result. He even had the damn lymph nodes biopsied six fucking times by a specialist! He was always told to quit drinking and change his lifestyle, but Bradley only heard the words, "possibility of schwannoma or neurofibroma." That was the only diagnosis he would accept.

He clung to the idea that he couldn't work, exercise, or go for a twenty-minute walk. He tried to apply for short-term disability, but his family doctor denied him that after a follow-up. Instead, he prescribed antidepressants, anti-anxiety medication, a sleep aid, and medication to manage the acute pain from the lymph nodes attached to his nerves in his left leg. He told Bradley to make changes in his lifestyle; he told him to quit smoking and drinking, and to work on his mental health. He also recommended Bradley see a counsellor and nutritionist.

No matter what was suggested, Bradley fought the idea that his drinking was the problem. He just took the drugs prescribed to him and moped around in the dark. The sun would be shining, but instead of enjoying the warmth of summer, he would be inside with the curtains drawn, playing video games. This got so bad I suspected mental illness on top of all his other battles. In fact, Bradley struggled severely with depression but refused my offer of help. He distracted himself by being the helper but would never allow others to help him. This wore him out even more.

In May 2020, Bradley received a letter with the news he had been accepted into a Bachelor of Education program that would train him to become a high school teacher. As excited as we were, I had major concerns. Bradley had only been sober for five months. After the last separation, I promised myself that I would be open and honest about everything. I explained carefully that I thought school would make matters worse. His health wasn't where it needed to be. He still wasn't sleeping and was struggling to find energy on a daily basis. I felt strongly that his mental and physical health should take precedence over any new endeavours.

I found even deeper courage and expressed my concerns about the state of our relationship. My trust had been broken and rebuilding that trust needed to be placed second behind his health. My word for this year was *truth*. Everything I said was indeed true and the power it held stood as a choice before him. I hoped he would see my love and concern for him. I prayed that he would take accountability and come to the truth. I hit home when I bluntly told him I feared school would be a distraction and that he wouldn't be able to handle all that the program would demand. I told him the reason he never finished anything was because he was ignoring his health. Our union, our home, and our family were all on thin ice. We needed each other and more time. School could wait a little longer. If he wanted to rebuild my trust, he needed to get healthy. He needed to understand and come to the same conclusion. Only then would he be able to be the best student and teacher possible.

What happened next was something I had become all too familiar with. He had a certain look when you said something that was true, but he wasn't ready to hear. He unleashed his wrath, shooting from the hip with hurt. "You are not taking this away from me!" he yelled spitefully. It was pretty much a "fuck you."

Old Elisha would have looked down and cried in defeat. I knew he would try to punish me with isolation, making me walk on eggshells until he got his way. I would end up tortured by his manipulation tactics and left in a puddle of my own self pity. Bradley's cruelty always destroyed my peace. The things he would say left me broken and alone. I often would crash and barely be able to take care of myself, let alone the children. All because I was trying to save him. My biggest fear was that his sober streak would end. I knew I couldn't go another round with Gollum.

I looked him dead straight in the eye, and without a flinch, as lovingly, kindly, and softly as I could, I replied, "I am making this possible for you by giving you my best! Can you honestly say the same?"

Thank fuck for wisdom. I walked out of the room and left him standing there in complete shock and silence. He didn't say a single word. I had waited so long to be heard and finally, I had made my stand. I knew what my best was in all this. Who do you think was going to support his ass? Who was going to pay his tuition? Who was going to cook, clean, and take charge of everything? Who was going to make his lunches and buy him a new wardrobe for his new career? Most importantly, who knew how to love him and look out for his best interests? Me!

I am strong, and no one needed to tell me how to truly love and live, and how to be an example for others to follow, including this man. When everything and everyone pushed him away, I stayed by his side with discipline and truth. I challenged him to be the man deep down he wanted to be and to reach for his greater purpose. I gave Bradley unlimited honour because I saw how capable he was as a man, best friend, husband, and father. I didn't punish him for his past mistakes and my actions spoke louder than ever on this. I brought him home when he was severely sick and nursed him through his detoxification. I stayed up with him all night, rubbing his legs and arms, trying to ease his restlessness. He would take long showers to ease the pain of his withdrawal symptoms—so long he ended up sitting on the floor of the shower stall so he could let the warm water wash over him for hours. I would be right there with him, sitting outside the shower, on the floor, holding his hand.

All of this I did knowing he had failed after just a few months out there alone. The women, drugs, alcohol abuse, and mountains of debt—the minute I brought him home I bore it all again. I feared he would use me, because the truth is he knew he couldn't do any of this without my support. I refused to live my life in fear of this disease and the man I loved. I saw his worth and raised him in love every day to it. Tough, real love. I was hard on him because I had to be. It was time I stopped doubting my truth.

Linda: 5; Bradley: 3.

I am accountable and responsible for fitting
with the correct cu̇
not fitting curriculum with the correct st.

(From an essay Bradley wrote wh
the Bachelor of Education program, September 2(

SIX

In the movie *After Earth*, Will Smith's character, Cypher Raige, says, "Danger is very real, but fear is a choice." All I was asking was for Bradley to see reason and understand that his health was at risk. Fear prevented Bradley from admitting that he was an addict, but he needed to focus on staying sober because his life depended on it. The risk of him slipping because of the inevitable stress of school was very real, but in the end he went. I made my peace with my doubts and stood back to observe, leaving it all in his hands. I encouraged him, often by participating in his work. I did anything I could to keep him healthy and his spirits high.

I had never seen Bradley so happy. He was eager to start his new career and be a part of more children's lives. He was born to be a father figure and raise others up; he was such an intelligent man. He could write flawlessly, using big fancy words, and created an everlasting flow of authenticity in his writing assignments. Bradley was always adored by everyone and the most popular person. His quick wit and drive to lead helped him excel in the classroom, and with his peers. Many looked up to him. I was able

`ile he attended school—a devot-
ake his dream a reality.
ew out, and he wore his glasses. At
spectacles forward onto his nose and
ds with his eyebrows arched and wrinkles
head. Anytime he did this, which was very
w glasses, I instantly saw his father. He looked
n. He sounded like him as well.
s relationship with his father was strained. He had
ntact with him as a teenager, spent summers and holi-
th him, and shared time over many phone calls as he grew
a man. Even so, I noticed he would often put his guard up
hen speaking to his father. He could never be himself. He
was always changing his tone or lying about something insig-
nificant, just to gain his father's approval. Bradley really struggled to fit in. He expressed at times that no matter what he made
of himself, he would always feel unsure of who his father wanted
him to be. He wanted to know his dad, but he admitted that
they didn't make the time to get to know one another. There was
always distance and division between these men—many words
were left unspoken. Bradley pushed even harder to show his father the man he was: a follower of God, a father, a partner, and
a scholar. He really wanted his dad to see the value of his studies.

In the summer of 2020, Bradley and I traveled to visit his father. On the way back home, I thought it was time to talk about
their relationship; I wanted to try to help Bradley rebuild what
he felt he had lost so long ago. When we were on a drive together
was the best time to reach Bradley. He couldn't escape, but he
also felt safe to express what was in his heart. I placed my hand
on his, and I started the conversation.

"Do you love your father?" I asked. Bradley always knew my

train of thought. Of course, I knew Bradley loved his father, but I was trying to get him to open up, to dig deeper by opening his heart to the truth. He made some quick, witty, and sarcastic remark. I knew this was his way of dodging the question, to cover up his pain with avoidance. What he said next was what needed to be said: those words that are typically left unspoken between a boy and his father.

"I don't know how to love him."

I made sure to give his words some space and not be so quick to reply. He needed time to process what he had finally said out loud. The thing with Bradley, at least when he was sober, was that he never blamed anyone but himself. He took accountability before throwing someone else under the bus. In fact, he often sacrificed himself to bear more burden. He knew his relationship with his father lacked due to his own selfishness. In one of Bradley's journal entries, he openly confessed his brokenness, expressing that he understood why he isn't loved. "How can anyone love a monster? I am unlovable," he wrote.

After the longest forty-five minutes of my life, I finally broke the silence. "It doesn't matter if you don't know how to love him. What matters most is you are worthy of his love."

When he was in a vulnerable state, Bradley often needed to be protected from himself. He trusted me more than anyone and knew I would make sure he understood his worth. I told him that people rarely admitted that they didn't know how to do something. It was always easier to blame someone else for their lack of self-worth and inability to escape their issues; it was hard to take responsibility and try to move forward.

I know now that Bradley didn't know how to love his father because he struggled daily to love himself. Ultimately, this meant he chose not to forgive himself. He forgave little therefore he loved little. With an unforgiving mindset and a hardened heart, Bradley condemned himself to being an unlovable monster. Someone with an addiction can do a lot of wrong making it hard to love them. It doesn't make it wrong to love them, but it does make it hard to understand their choices and the pain they cause.

It broke my heart to think this man didn't think he deserved to be loved. I told him he was a good man, worthy of love and so much more. I knew that my words would seem empty until he found truth inside his own will and heart. At that point, I was crying after expressing how much love and greatness I saw in him. He had been sick for so long that he had lost sight of his purpose—all he saw was his pain. I wept for him as he was my equal and my everything. What hurt him, broke me. Looking up at him with tears streaming down my face, I asked, "What would I do if I ever lost you Bradley?" I will never forget his words. I replay the conversation over and over every day. It was the way he said it, without hesitation and full of conviction.

"You will be just fine," he replied, without looking away from my gaze.

Linda: 5; Bradley: 4.

I will never forget the day I took a photo of Bradley. It was the first photo I ever took. I don't take pictures of anyone—or anything for that matter. I have always believed they are locked into place in my memory, and I prefer to share those memories by talking about the places I've been, the things I've seen, and the people I've met. But this time, it was different. The same voice I heard when I was lying on the bathroom floor after Bradley had left spoke again. It was the same soft whisper in my ear when I saw Bradley for the first time. The words came loud and clear:

"Take the picture!" I shied away from the idea, doubt flooding my mind. Bradley hated having his picture taken, and he knew I hated taking pictures. How would I explain this? At that moment, I looked up and what I saw next cannot be conveyed in mere words. He was beautiful. I was mesmerized, caught in a trance, in disbelief at the perfection of the moment. There he was, sitting at the kitchen table, eating a bowl of homemade chicken noodle soup. He was taking a short lunch break from school. He was wearing his glasses, had styled his curly hair, and was sporting the shirt we had designed together when I had agreed to sponsor his billiards team with my small business. It was honestly like a dream or a movie set. He represented everything he loved. I pulled my lady balls out and got my phone in hand.

I made sure to choose the right camera setting to best reflect the moment. I was trying to find the words to coax him to look at me without giving away that I was about to take his picture. I wanted to capture the moment just as it was. Then I knew what needed to be said. "My love?" I held the phone in place, a nervous but soft smile formed on my lips. He took in my eyes and smiled back.

Click!

He never asked to see the photo. I wasn't going to push my luck. I fell in love with his beauty. It was so much more than a photo. He was perfect: healed, happy, peaceful, and serene. He never knew I made it the wallpaper on my phone. He never knew what it truly meant to me. He was so beautiful. He was the very essence of freedom. He had surrendered. All things were possible. Bradley was set free and given a new life—a fresh start and a new beginning. He was changing and transforming. He started to live freely and to open his life in love. Salvation was his truth.

Bradley had to choose a word that would resonate with him

as he went through the teacher training program. What follows is the essay he wrote for that assignment.

The best word I can think of to lead me through 2021 and beyond is *surrender*.

If you know me at all, you know I have a strong, opinionated personality. Even to a fault I will stick with what I know until I am shown, with evidence, that another idea or opinion can contribute to my overall understanding. Now, don't confuse this with arrogance or stubbornness. It may seem that way, and sometimes it is, but I try hard to appreciate the value of those around me. I struggle to hear when my understanding is infected by my personal interpretation.

When I disagree with something, it is usually because I have put some serious thought into whatever it is we are discussing. Perhaps I won't answer and just listen. That's me questioning your intentions with whatever it is you're sharing. Making mental notes to go and find out whether what you said, especially the way you said it, is true or false. I like this part of my personality and I don't want to change it.

Therefore, I must surrender. If I don't want to change this part of myself moving forward into a teaching career, I am not going to be a good teacher or be able to collaborate effectively with my peers and mentors. Adding authority to a personality characteristic like this, especially one that I don't want to change, could be dangerous and cause more harm than good within a classroom of subordinate students. Pair that dynamic with a quick wit and ability to talk and I will find myself in uncomfortably charged conversations or class discussions.

As Kung Fu master Bruce Lee once said in an interview, "Be like water." I want to fill the empty space I am in to become a part of that space, humbling myself and relinquishing control to others around me. My purpose moving forward in this career, in my life as a father, friend, and husband, and as a mentor, peer, or associate is to serve with my knowledge, opinion, quick wit, and charisma. I will accept opinions or ideas outside of myself and work hard to understand why that person, in this context, holds that perspective. I'm still going to want evidence, not to dissuade anyone, but because I appreciate the knowledge being shared with me.

Bradley would never admit it, but I was his inspiration for this paper. I challenged him in ways no one had the courage to. In fact, when times were good, we made a great pair, embracing one another's wisdom and respecting each other's ideas. We held on to that gift as two people, two minds, and two hearts. The result: we became "like water." We were together as one identity. When two people come with love to serve one another, they are stronger together.

I remember reading his paper in front of him with a smile on my lips. "What are you smirking about, Linda?" he asked. I stood up and handed the paper back to him and started for the door. I turned on one heel, my eyes meeting his.

"I wonder who encouraged you, my darling, to change and seek the meaning of surrender?" I replied, laughing as the words left my mouth.

"It's not a competition, Linda!"

"Now Mr. Kempster!" I snapped back. I stood square, facing him, my arms folded across my body. "Are you questioning my intentions? Are you making mental notes to see if what I say is true or false? Or is this just you being arrogant with a side plate of stubbornness?!" He leapt from his chair and started chasing me upstairs. I screamed and moved my ass as fast as I could up the stairs shouting back at him, "Be like water!"

Linda: 6; Bradley: 4.

This is my happiest memory of Bradley. He knew everything was a competition to me. By observing his quick wit and sense of humour, I developed my own and loved to use it against him. We created so much laughter together, teasing and poking fun at each other. There was no romance with Bradley. Anytime I would pour out my soul, he would always reply in some funny and sarcastic way, never taking me seriously. In fact, he would make even more fun of me by calling me Linda. This is why this story is my favourite memory of us. It was the one time he poured out his soul to me; he was in such a vulnerable state, wanting to do well at school. And I pounced at the opportunity to get him back for all the times he got me. It was quality over quantity. This was my moment. The best part was that we laughed together, and he admitted it was a good one. My all-time favourite thing to do for this man was to make him laugh at my own expense, which wasn't very often as he always beat me to it. No other man has ever made me laugh like he did.

That's not true. I didn't know at the time, but our son has all of Bradley's quick wit, charisma, sense of humour, and sarcasm. He makes me laugh, even more.

I wonder if I am enough. Am I enough as a father and husband? Some things I know I fall short on. I struggle knowing why I feel this way. Confused, lost, neutral, unsure— settling my mind to accept this life. So many questions that are unanswered and will never be answered. Sitting in silence waiting for healing, praying for guidance, receiving some answers, but wanting more understanding of my suffering.

(From Bradley's journal, January 2021)

SEVEN

"Be gentle, Elisha. Be still in me." A soft whisper spoke as I sat in a nearby park and took in the sunrise of a new day. *Gentle*: my word for 2021. All my fears had come true. It was January 2021, and Bradley was crashing again. He was cycling back into drinking and the disease was taking a final stand. School was slipping away; his assignments were late, and he had stopped showing up for classes. Money was disappearing and unexplained costs were accumulating. Bradley's mental stability was in the scariest state I'd ever seen. He had manipulated me into shaving off all his beautiful, long curls. I felt awful after I'd done it, and he looked scarier than ever with his bald head.

After Bradley's hair cut, I cried. It broke my heart to see him that way, with part of his identity gone. I wept, not because of the hair itself, but because I knew then that his illness had taken over. He was sicker than ever and fading away faster than I had anticipated. He was so depressed, irritable, and isolated. He would disappear into his man cave and sit there in the dark with the television on all day. I was concerned for his mental state and would try to encourage him and motivate him, but he would just respond with hurtful words to weaken my efforts. "You're useless to me; go and find some intelligence elsewhere!" he would yell.

The isolation was the worst. I would beg him not to punish me with silence, but he would explode into one of his drinking fits and leave for days without a word. Eventually, he would come home drunk or hungover yet still with enough energy to yell, "I can't fucking stand you! You suck the very life out of me!"

He would lie to me about his migraines, saying they'd appeared because he had forgotten to take his medications. There was no fucking chance in hell that he would forget to take those pills. It was clear to me that the drinking was the culprit. By this point, Bradley's physical health was deteriorating. I watched him gain anywhere from two to four pounds a week. His last weigh in was just shy of 310 pounds.

I will never forget what I found when I went to clean up the dishes in the man cave one afternoon. He was asleep and looked like he'd spilled something all over himself. He was soaked in sweat. I went closer to touch his forehead; it was ice cold. I could hear him breathing—it was loud and deep. I placed my head on his chest to hear his heartbeat. It was difficult due to the snoring, but I could hear a faint beat. I looked down at his belly and saw something yellow coming out of his belly button. My curiosity got the better of me and I went to smell it. To this day I will never forget that smell. You would think that as a mother who has changed diapers and been thrown up on, I'd have seen and smelled everything, but this was unlike anything I had ever experienced before. I stood back with my hand over my mouth and took in the whole sight of him. His skin was pale and yellow—not the soft golden tan he usually was. He didn't look like Bradley anymore. I almost dropped the dishes and bolted out of the room, but I was afraid to wake him. I barely made the stairs before I dropped everything and started to weep.

This was bad. It was the worst I had ever seen. I wondered how I would convince him that he was really sick and that he needed to see a doctor—immediately! For so long, I'd tried to gently encourage him to go for walks, get fresh air, and eat better. I would make healthy food for him, and it made me feel better to know at least he was eating well. None of it worked. He would eat the healthy meal I made for him, but an hour later he'd stuff his face with crap. He would make any excuse not to move, often blaming the pain in his leg. He'd just sit there and play video games. I remember saying to him, "I am not a doctor, but I know your history and habits better than any other person and I am telling you this is the one body you have. Please take care of it."

I had devoted myself to improving his health. I had spent hours preparing healthy meals. I had tried to lead by example and encouraged him to join me for walks, to do yoga, and to train with me. This was all running through my head as I sat there on the stairs, weeping. His body couldn't take another cycle. The sickness had developed into a severe illness. What more could I do? The last time I mentioned "addiction" and "alcohol" in the same sentence, he destroyed me. I couldn't go through that again. I didn't have the energy for this seemingly endless fight. I couldn't disappear again and melt into nothingness. The children needed me. *I* needed me.

I sat on those stairs for what seemed like a lifetime, trying to find hope, trying to think of something I could do. The truth was I had done everything I could do to save this man. I had given him a new life and a choice. The problem was he wouldn't come to the truth. Then in that moment, I heard a song my mother used to sing. She had learned it from her mother. The words echoed in my mind and imprinted on my soul. I sang them out loud: "He will never change if I stay." I had stayed for ten years, and these words were clearer than ever. Would I find the courage to finally leave? I prayed for a sign, repeating my word for this year: *gentle*. Be gentle—gentle in spirit, gentle in mind, gentle in body. Gentle.

I knew more than ever that I needed help. I had to confront my situation. The place I had called home wasn't a home anymore and hadn't been for some time. I no longer felt safe there. Bradley had begun to insult me, calling my worth as a mother, a wife, and even a human being into question. He blamed me for his drinking problem. When he was drunk, Bradley had become not only verbally and psychologically abusive, he was now sexually abusive towards me, often forcing me to have sex against my will. I knew that my health was at risk, and the fear of further abuse was sending me into a depression. I began to have thoughts of suicide again.

I knew what I had to do. I started to build my strength and find the courage to leave. I started training. I trained my mind with wisdom to battle anxiety; I trained my body with exercise to help with stress; I trained my spirit with prayer to help with what was to come. This time, I was getting out for good. I knew this wasn't going to be easy, but it was time to start listening to that inner voice, my gut and, most importantly, my spirit within me. I found the thing that I'd lost so long ago: hope. Hope was before me. I just had to grab it and never let it go. I had to manifest that hope with my actions.

I became a ghost to Bradley. Unless it had to do with family or business, I was completely distant. I had to be. Conversations were kept to a bare minimum. If he entered a room, I would leave it. I didn't trust him but even more, I didn't trust myself. I was so vulnerable in my preparation for what I knew had to happen. I still loved him, but I wouldn't allow that to cloud my judgement. I had been given a new path, and I was going to follow it. I trusted that if I had been given a new direction, then he would have one too. I had given this man everything I could. Now, I had to stand back knowing I would not be a part of his life any longer. In fact, his path was no longer my business, nor my concern.

"Let go the people who are not prepared to love you. This is the hardest thing you will have to do in your life and it will also be the most important thing you do." During this difficult time, I found strength and comfort in these words, written by Brianna Wiest in her essay "This Year, Let Go of the People Who Aren't Ready to Love You." I came across her words one afternoon and memorized them. I had prayed for a sign, and I didn't get just one sign, I got a total of three! This was the first one. I printed these words out and taped them to my kitchen cupboard. To this day, I read them every morning!

A client and dear friend of mine came for an appointment shortly after I had made my decision to leave Bradley. I knew I wanted to go, but I was struggling to find the strength to finally leave. I was afraid of Bradley but even more fearful of looking over my shoulder. He wouldn't last long without me. His acts of cruelty were always the worst when he knew I wasn't totally within his grasp. I had to choose myself this time and leave without turning back no matter what, but I honestly didn't know how to implement it. How could I find the courage to move forward for the rest of my life without Bradley? I expressed my concerns for what lay ahead to my friend. I knew what was coming and was fully aware that my fear might overpower my choice. I told her I was afraid of Bradley.

"You're not afraid of him, you fear the disease behind the man," she corrected me. She nailed it. I depended on and trusted her words more than anything as she had also been a victim of this awful disease. The only difference was she was twenty-five years ahead of me and in her late fifties. I asked her why she hadn't left, why she hadn't let go and started living her life free of her sick husband. With tears in her eyes, she simply said, "I can't." She explained to me that she couldn't leave because she would owe him so much in alimony. She had found a compromise and had constructed a safe haven for herself where she lived a separate life from him. She admitted it was not ideal, and she would prefer to be completely free—free to be loved—but it wasn't an option for her. In hearing this, and seeing her cry more than ever, I grabbed her hand and cried with her.

"What would you tell a younger version of yourself who was in the same situation?" I asked. I will never forget her words. I will never forget the pain and sorrow in her eyes as she looked upon me.

"Get out now!" she replied, without hesitation. She was my future. I saw it with my own eyes: what I would become—alone and forever trapped. There it was: my second sign. I dared not hide or run. It was time to face my own addiction: suffering. Now I had to stop and face my shit.

I was ecstatic when a couple of girlfriends invited me out for dinner and drinks one evening in March 2021. I'd been training and working long hours, nonstop. This was a nice treat and a surprise. I had worked really hard on myself and had actually started building relationships outside of my home. I was thrilled to say I had girlfriends. Around the same time, Bradley finished his first term and his first practicum to become a schoolteacher. I was surprised. Based on his situation at the beginning of the year, I was convinced he was going to fail. I don't know what made him turn it around. Maybe he realized I was planning to leave him. Maybe that scared him. Whatever the reason, somehow, he had pushed through and got his act together. He would graduate from his teaching program in December 2021. All he had left was his second term and the second practicum. We were both happy for each other.

He encouraged me to have a good time with my friends, but just as I was leaving, I saw it. There on the kitchen table was a six pack of beer. My heart started pounding and my legs went numb. My anxiety shot through the roof. I couldn't help but think, "The one time I get invited out and he has to drink?" Part of the reason I didn't go out or socialize with friends was because I didn't trust Bradley alone. So many times, I would come home to a situation or a disaster. I feared the pain of what was going to happen.

I felt my face flush when I saw the alcohol on the table. He saw it and started to try to soothe me. He told me everything was ok and that I didn't need to worry. I begged him not to drink until I got home, but he said he wanted to celebrate and play video games. He said he would text me and keep me posted throughout the evening. He gave me a half-hearted hug and a kiss on my forehead, and I left reluctantly. I had been ready to cancel my evening plans.

Pulling up outside the restaurant, I tried to gather myself together. I was still feeling butterflies in my stomach when I heard my phone receive a text message. It was from Bradley: "You deserve this; you have been working so hard and I am proud of you. Please have a good time with your girlfriends. Love you."

After receiving his message, I felt renewed. For the first time in a long time, he acknowledged my efforts and appreciated them. We hadn't spoken much lately and barely saw one another during the day at this point. We were sleeping separately. But all that resentment melted away with his message. Another hour into my evening he sent me another: "I hope you're enjoying your time, my love." This was heaven to my ears. He was present like he said he would be. He was there for me. This had seemed like an impossibility. I relaxed and started to be in the moment— sharing drinks and laughter.

Three hours into my evening, I messaged him to ask how his evening was going. No reply. Another hour went by, and I messaged I would be home soon. Before I left the restaurant, I checked my phone. Still no reply. I hadn't heard from him since 7:30 p.m. It was now 10:00 p.m. A sick feeling melted all over my body. Something in my gut told me to get home.

I started crying the minute I found him. He was passed out on the living room floor, his keys, phone, and money spread across the floor. He was on his back snoring more loudly than ever. I took in the scene: a beer can on the table, three left in the fridge. I knew beer hadn't done this. Praying I was wrong, I opened the freezer. There it was, the weapon itself, with a gold label: Honey Jack Daniels. I grabbed the two-six bottle in anger. It was all gone but a tablespoon. I slammed the freezer door. I was so angry. He had lied to me by hiding this bottle. I remembered asking him why he didn't use our account when he bought beer. Duh! It was because he didn't just buy beer. I flashbacked to his words: "Everything is going to be ok. Nothing to worry about." I screamed in anger. I remembered feeling his kiss and half-assed embrace. No wonder he couldn't look me in the eye. Now, slowly, with tears running down my face, I entered the living room. I seriously contemplated leaving his fat ass on the floor. Instead, to get back at him in a way, I picked up his shit first. When I grabbed his phone, I saw a message. I opened it. Yep. Surprise, surprise. Gollum was back, and he was cheating. I sat back down and stared at Bradley. Here were more tears. Here was more pain. More. More. More. I finally said out loud, after so long keeping it all in, "Where are you? I am so fucking tired. I am just so tired."

I grabbed all the courage and love I could to wake him. Carefully and softly, I said his name and touched his chest. I added more pressure to my touch and deepened my voice to rouse him. When he finally opened his eyes, his pupils were so tiny. He was completely lost. He looked past me and didn't even see me. His eyes were empty.

In the end, it wasn't the cheating, lying, manipulation, abuse, pain, or even the drinking that made me determined to get out. It was his eyes. His eyes were my third sign and my last. My Bradley, the man I had been in love with for my entire life, was no longer. All that was left was the disease.

Troubles have built for a long while now.
I feel I am in the lowest spot I could be in.
There is little worry or fear.
I gave my troubles of this world to my Father.
He gives me peace every day.
His plan is taking hold of me.
I cannot see it yet, but I know it's coming.

(From Bradley's journal, February 2021)

EIGHT

I would not go to him. Not this time nor ever again. I listened to him get sick for four days straight—endless sounds of throwing up and the smell that it produced. I didn't hold his hand when he had one of his long showers. I stayed as far from him as I could. He needed to learn about accountability and what being alone with his disease would be like. He needed to see that the illness made him weaker by the day and sicker every night. He needed to admit to all the lies and manipulation of Gollum. He needed to witness it because his very life depended on it. It broke my heart to see him in this state, now more than ever as I knew what needed to be done.

I kept my distance downstairs, cleaning and doing inventory for the business. Bradley avoided me just as much as I did him. When I heard the basement door open one day, my heart started pounding. Bradley sat in the salon wash sink chair, but I couldn't look at him. I just continued with my task. Ten minutes went by, and nothing was said. Another ten, and still nothing. I knew he was waiting to be punished, to be given consequences, to be asked to make me promises he couldn't keep. He was waiting for me to give the same speech I had always given in the past, so I could watch him clean up his act for a little while only to crash again and repeat the same cycle. He expected to have the same pointless talk, making me the controlling, mean, bad guy. I broke the silence with a question, hoping he would take accountability.

"What is it that I can do for you Bradley?"

Ten minutes went by and then another ten. Nothing was said. This made me angry. I refused to allow him to play the victim. I could feel his self-pity like a weight on my shoulders. How many times had he used this tactic when he'd really fucked up? He would go from Gollum to Eeyore in the flick of a switch. I wanted to harness my anger and scream at him for all the bullshit he had put me through for all these years. He had *never* listened to me. He had consistently and selfishly taken from our family and me in particular. I'd lied to everyone for him. I was always making excuses to cover up why we were late or were a no-show to life outside our house. I wanted to let out the rage deep inside me and crush him for all the pain he caused me—all the drunken mess, piss, shit, and vomit I'd been subjected to. I blamed him mostly for making me keep this secret from the children and the rest of our family. The years of torture were to blame for my unhappiness. I wanted to treat him the way he had always treated me. I felt so denied, rejected, and most of all, worthless. I really wanted to hit him for all the pain he'd subjected me to. I had given him everything he had asked for. I had made it possible for him to have such an amazing life with me at his side. I had given him all the love and support I could. I had persevered, guiding him back to his roots and morals with truth. Then my mind stopped. I had anger right there on my lips and tongue, aimed and ready to vomit all of my agony onto him. But then I heard that voice again, loud and clear: "Gentle!"

Gentle in spirit and slow to speak, I took a deep breath in and out. It was time. I needed every ounce of my strength in this moment—this is what I had trained for. Without eye contact, as I knew it wasn't time yet, and with my back facing him, I found wisdom in my words. Softly, I said, "Bradley, I have outgrown you and your lifestyle. It has been just shy of ten years and nothing has changed. I have to let you go! For far too long I have been made to believe that letting go would mean I was a failure. I thought I couldn't face another failed marriage. I realize how very wrong I have been. Letting go is a declaration of how much love I have for *myself*, for my own well-being. You are a ten out of ten: a beautiful man, a wonderful, loving father, and a promising teacher. You have been an enduring husband, but all this has slipped from your hands because you refuse to acknowledge the truth. I have never asked you for an apology even though I deserve one. To me, true love means being able to see past my own pain and to know you can't give an apology. In fact, you refuse to give one. You're never going to change. You will never change if I stay." I turned to face him. He was still sitting in the chair staring at his hands. "Look at me!" I demanded. My voice was deep and firm. What I said next was a warning. "I will never pick you up off the floor again …" I paused. Tears began to glaze my eyes as they searched for his. I wondered, "Do I dare say these words?" Once again, the soft and gentle voice spoke. "I will never pick you up off the floor again; you must pick yourself up." I looked into the very soul of the man I loved, and said, "If you don't acknowledge your addiction and start looking after yourself, the next time, you will be dead." His eyes never moved from mine. "You are sick, Bradley. It's time to be a man and fix this. You have got a problem, so deal with it and fix it. I *won't* have it in my life anymore! It's time I let you go."

I didn't realize it then, but I would cling to these words for years to come; they would give me peace. I knew I did everything I could to save this man. In that moment, I forgave him and that was the key to my freedom. I learned that you have to let go of anger towards people who have wronged you if you want to be free and get on with your life.

The next morning, I was getting ready in the bathroom for work. Bradley entered and leaned on the wall. Without eye contact he said, "I am sorry for lying to you that night I drank and for stealing money." He left the minute the word "sorry" hit his lips. No tears came from me.

The next evening, I was sitting watching television and, once again, he entered the room. He looked down, unable to look me in the eye. I muted the television. "I am sorry you had to find me the way you did. I know that hurt you." Just as before, after he said sorry, he left. This broke my heart as I saw more than ever his pain in those words coming from his mouth. I knew right then and there that no one had ever apologized to him. Again, I had no tears, but my heart ached deeply.

On the third day, in the evening, I was reading in my bedroom with the door closed. I heard a knock. He opened the door but stood on the threshold for what seemed like ages. Eventually, this time, his eyes met mine. "I am sorry I hurt you by being with another woman and for all the times I have cheated on you."

Now it was my turn to look away. Tears streamed down my face. He knew this one hurt the most. Most of my trauma and pain stemmed from his betrayal. He reached for the door to close it. My voice chased after the door before it closed. "I forgive you Bradley!"

That was last time I ever spoke to Bradley.

He didn't hear me, and the door closed. I was shaking in

grief. This issue had destroyed us long ago. Bradley's last indiscretion took everything from us and changed our future together. Bradley had contracted an STI—an infection that was permanent. I had managed to end all sexual intimacy long before due to his addiction; however, this ended our union all together. I wouldn't sleep with him but more importantly, I wouldn't share my spirit with his broken one. Our souls were divided. Even after hearing the news of his infection about a year before, I still stayed with him. I found other ways to fulfill my needs. I was just so thankful he didn't pass the infection on to me. I was clean and safe, and moving forward in gratitude. Bradley couldn't face the shame of it all. Sometimes—not very often—he'd look at me and I could tell the guilt was destroying his very being. He had failed as a man to protect and provide for the woman who had done nothing but protect and provide for him. Despite the betrayals and the abuse, I had remained by his side. I had forgiven him and found peace with all of it.

Bradley had never apologized before—not once in the years we had been together. His heart had been hardened against these words due to his pain from others hurting him. It took him three days to give three separate apologies. I had hoped he would come to see the truth in my words. I had hoped he'd ask for help and know what he had to do next to better his life. Unfortunately, that was not the case. His drinking increased and his mental stability was deteriorating. He was Eeyore during the day and Gollum at night. His actions spoke the loudest to me. He stayed all day and night in his cave, missing classes and assignments. The smell gave away the alcohol consumption, though I never knew how much. He was up all night and barely slept in the day. He would put on a show by calling family and disguising his real self as best as he could. As I suspected, he couldn't stand by his apologies. This all took place within a month of my last conversation with him. Nothing had changed. I had been right all along.

I notified my family of our final separation. I locked down my finances in fear Gollum would act out again. When I told him he needed to leave by the end of the month, he made threats about the house. At this point, I was telling him anything he wanted to hear via email just to get him out of the house. I said I'd pay him whatever he asked for. That was a white lie on my part. He was a liability and I needed him to leave. This was my top priority for the sake of the kids and our home.

On Wednesday March 31, 2021, I called his mother to tell her I had decided to leave her son. I didn't explain why, as I knew deep down, she was well aware of the problem. Many words were left unspoken, except the most important message I wanted to leave her with: that I loved her. No matter what happened, she would always be welcome in my home. The last separation was so hurtful and ugly, I wouldn't subject her to that pain again, not by my hand. I wanted to reassure her that my family would always be her family, and that there would be no repeats of the past when it came to Bradley and me. I honoured and loved her as my own mother. I wanted to do right by her and to warn her that her son was not well.

On April 2, 2021—Good Friday—I sat down with the children and with their stepmother and biological father in their home. Together, we took turns comforting the children. I felt so embarrassed that I was putting them through this again. Now, the five of us had to piece it all together again. I couldn't tell the children why. I could only say that their stepfather was very sick, and we could not be in his life anymore. My daughter, just ten years old at the time, only saw the good in Bradley. My son was silent, his spirit broken. Deep down, he knew this was coming. He had witnessed the same behaviour and energy within our home. He trusted me. A thirteen-year-old boy stood by his mother's choice, even though he didn't fully understand it.

Together we comforted one another through the Easter weekend. I wouldn't allow the children near Bradley. He wasn't their father at this time.

On Sunday April 4, 2021, he left presents for both the children. This made it so hard as my daughter kept begging to hug and cuddle with him. I allowed her to say thank you and to give him a hug, but I kept my eye on them. I saw him grab her chin and lift it up to kiss her forehead. He said the words he always said to her: "I love you, baby girl!"

My son was angry and disappointed with the gifts, saying that he really just wanted Bradley. He'd rather have a father that would stay and be around than the gifts. Bradley gave him a pat on the back while my son struggled to hold back his tears, blinking rapidly so the tears didn't fall onto his cheek. Before disappearing back into his cave, Bradley said, "I love you, my boy. Everything will be ok."

Later that evening, after I had tucked the kids into my king-sized bed, I went downstairs to prepare my workout gear for the next day. I saw a piece of paper with a blue sticky note on top of it. It was a marriage licence application. The sticky note read: "How committed I am."

"You have got to be fucking kidding me!" I thought. I raged over that fucking note. How inappropriate; it was a replay of our engagement. So many promises made but not kept. It was such an obvious attempt to manipulate me. Full fucking cycle. "How committed I am." The truth was there was no commitment, not even to himself. I made my mind up to break the silence and have one last conversation with him. I wanted to point to my ring finger and tell him *I* was the one who was committed and always had been. I didn't need a fucking piece of paper to prove that. I wanted to put him up on the stand to confess that this wasn't love—this was attachment. He was just afraid he couldn't do everything that he wanted without me. He didn't last four months on his own without asking for money, food, and warmth. I was going to make it my mission to put self-pitying Eeyore to rest with a smack of reality. I wanted to punch Eeyore in his donkey nut sack. I stomped upstairs to find his ass.

I came to the kitchen window and saw him outside, on his phone, smoking a cigarette. I watched carefully how his body moved and the way he was talking. I knew he was talking to his mother and that he was drinking. I had made a rule long before, a boundary of sorts: I never talked to him when he was under the influence. Ever. In this moment, as I watched him put on another show for a family member, convincing them all is well, I saw the illness take over. Looking down at the paper in my hands, I saw it was just another way for this narcissistic addict to gain control over my peace. I bowed my head right then and asked for wisdom; I let go of my anger and asked for God to send love his way. I feared for him so deeply at this time. I was so proud of myself as I walked away and joined my two beautiful babies. I fell asleep in their arms. The hardest thing I have ever done in my life was doing what was right.

On April 5, Easter Monday, I laid in bed for hours. I hadn't slept well at all. I finally pulled myself together and got dressed in my workout gear around 5:30 a.m. I headed downstairs to start my routine. I noticed the salon bathroom light was on and Bradley's man cave door was open. I quietly closed his door so I would not disturb him. I took a deep breath, dreading what kind of mess I would find in the bathroom. I opened the door and saw two legs. Spider web veins of blue ran up one of his calves. I screamed—it was Bradley! He was lying in a fetal position beside the toilet. I pulled his pants up. His face was all blue and clear liquid was coming out of his mouth and nose. He wasn't breathing. I grabbed my phone and dialed 911. The operator answered and told me to stay calm and that it was imperative that I roll Bradley over on to his back so I could start compressions. I am a strong woman, and at that time I was in pretty good shape, but for the life of me, I couldn't roll him over. The 911 dispatcher kept encouraging me to try until the paramedics came. I kept calling out his name. "Bradley. Come on baby. Please . . ."

By the seventh try, I got him over onto his back and started CPR. The dispatcher made it clear that I should not attempt mouth to mouth resuscitation. I was in such a state of shock I listened to the dispatcher's every word. I kept pushing harder and harder, faster and faster, to bring some sort of movement back into my Bradley. I swore I broke something in my efforts. Tears and snot covered my hands. I started hyperventilating and the dispatcher was trying to keep me calm but pushing me to focus on the task at hand: Bradley.

"Please baby, please please please," I wailed in pain.

Ten minutes later, I heard the paramedics arrive; at the same time, I heard my son, awake, calling out my name. His voice was sharper and at a higher pitch than normal. He was scared. As any mother would, I rushed to protect my son; I stopped my compressions and ran to the stairs. He took in all of me and knew something was very wrong. "Mom! What is happening? Is it Dad? Why are . . .?"

I cut him off and told him to let the paramedics in. He froze. I shouted at him, tears streaming down my hot cheeks, and it made him jump. "I need you! Now! Be brave and let them in. Do *not* come downstairs!" I yelled, my eyes never leaving his. I returned to Bradley. There was no room to work on him in the bathroom, so a paramedic, two firefighters, and I moved Bradley into the main area of the basement. I stood back and away knowing I'd done all I could and watched six men work on Bradley. I heard someone behind me. I looked and there was my son, stunned.

I gathered him into my arms and took him upstairs. I grabbed my phone and called my parents. They heard the sense of panic and desperation in my voice and said they'd be on their way immediately. By now, my daughter was up due to all the commotion. Once again, I looked at my son. Barely breathing, my face stained with tears, and my body soaked in my own sweat, I said the hardest words I have ever had to say to him. "I cannot be with you right now. I need you to wait for me up here and take care of your sister. Grandpa and Grandma are on the way. Whatever happens, whatever you hear, stay upstairs. Do you understand me?" I made him say "yes" out loud. I called my mother again and screamed at her through the phone, "Where are you? I need you *here!*"

I went back downstairs to Bradley. By now, everyone was distant. No one was working on him. I noticed he was no longer blue, but he was very still. The male paramedic looked at me and said, "Unfortunately, Brad is dead."

My knees buckled and I fell to the floor. I slowly made my way to him. I held Bradley in my arms, caressing his head, stroking his cheek, and kissing his lips. He was so cold. I rocked back and forth repeating the word "no" out loud. "This can't be real. This is just a bad day, this is just a nightmare," I thought to myself. I closed my eyes, hoping I would wake up. I begged myself to wake up. Without realizing it, I started saying that out loud. "Wake up. Please. Wake up."

The men surrounding me just stared. Silence filled the room aside from a woman's cries for her beloved, now gone. Her whole world—her heart, her life, her everything—gone. Everything? No! I realized the children were upstairs, alone. I carefully placed Bradley down. Salty water from my tears covered his face. I leaned forward carefully to give him one last kiss. Running my hands though his hair, I whispered into his ear, "I will see you soon, my love."

*I want the children to know I wish
to see them grow as individuals, to be confident
that everything isn't easy, that they will make mistakes.
Mistakes aren't bad or good;
they are opportunities to learn about themselves
and the world around them.*

(From Bradley's journal, March 2021)

NINE

I ran upstairs to my children who I feared were all alone, not knowing what was happening. I entered the living room and saw a young man sitting with them. The firefighter and I exchanged looks and with a soft smile I mouthed the words "thank you." My children had never been alone.

"Mom, where is Dad?" my son asked.

I didn't answer the question. Instead, I began to shake as his light blue eyes recognized the truth. He just started to cry. I joined him. My daughter was very confused.

"Mom, I want to see Dad now!" Her innocent voice cracked through her tears.

I gathered them both up and held them still in my arms. I didn't want to tell these two precious children that their dad was dead. I felt the warmth of the sun come through the window. I felt it on my face and on the three of us. I grabbed both of their little faces in my hands. Their eyes filled with the same salty tears which then started to stream down their faces. Lifting their tiny eyes to mine, I said, "He is in heaven!"

My words were clear, and they knew what they meant. Their

cries became louder. Their hearts began to beat stronger and faster. They wouldn't let me go.

My parents had arrived soon after I had called my mother screaming in panic. I have never heard my father cry as loud as he did that day. His agony came through his cries for Bradley who had been like a son to him. He was in such disbelief. I will never forget my mother's face when they pulled up and got out of the car. I saw the sorrow in her eyes and her pain for me. She has always known the deep love I had for Bradley. She bore witness to the worst pain imaginable—her daughter's loss of the only man she'd ever loved.

The police and the coroner now started their duties. I grabbed my phone, gripping it tightly, and slowly dialed his mother's number. My father offered to call her instead, but I knew it had to be me. Trying hard to keep my voice still, I said, "Mom." I paused. I couldn't even speak. With that lingering pause, she knew something was wrong.

"Elisha, is everything ok?" she asked.

"You need to come to the house as soon as possible," I told her.

"Why? What is going on? Is it Bradley? Elisha, tell me!" I could tell she knew. A mother always knows.

"Bradley passed away this morning." I replied.

I felt sick to my stomach saying those words to her over the phone. I worried she'd crash driving to the house.

"Elisha, no! Elisha! No! No! No!" She wailed in pain. I heard her agony over the phone, her voice cracking just before she hung up.

I felt such an overwhelming sense of guilt over Bradley's passing. I know exactly why he died. The cops questioned me about Bradley's thoughts of suicide, and the family got aggressive about the very idea of it. The truth is, Bradley knew how sick he was, and every day he drank, he knew he was slowly killing himself. What is the difference between someone ending their life quickly and someone choosing a slow, painful death? I've known the truth all along. It was my job to keep it hidden—until that moment.

I pulled one of the police officers aside so I could speak with him privately, away from the family. I explained that Bradley's health—both mental and physical—hadn't been good for some time. I told him Bradley struggled with drinking, and that I believed he was an alcoholic with a substance abuse issue too. The police officer found some empty beer cans and medication. I told both officers that these things alone could not have done this. For Bradley to have been in the state I found him in, something more had to have been involved. They investigated further, but nothing more was found.

I started doubting myself. Was I wrong? Was I to blame for his death? Was I making shit up in my head about him being an alcoholic? Had I caused him to drink more due to my lies? The coroner couldn't determine the cause of death at the scene, and Bradley had to be sent away for an autopsy. She handed me a case number and told me to call in the next three days to follow up on the results.

Once everybody left, I took the kids to the park. I sat on the bench in the warm sun. I was so grateful the sun shone upon us that day. My parents tried to accompany us. They didn't want to leave me alone. It was nice to say "no" and not have any feelings of guilt. This was the start of many "no thank yous" as I began to set some boundaries.

I remember thinking it was crazy that we were sitting at the park, having lost so much just hours ago. Life around us still existed. Kids were playing and laughing, adults were having conversations, and the sun was shining ever so brightly. I will never forget that moment. I sat on a bench looking at my two children sitting by the riverbank, hanging their feet over the edge. I saw my daughter lean her head into her brother, and without any hesitation, he wrapped his arm around her. The voice came again, but this time from inside me. "Take the picture."

We stayed there for hours together, soaking in the warmth of the sun and the comfort of being together. My daughter decided now was the time to be honest about what she felt she needed the most. "Mom?" she asked.

"Yes Hailey," I replied with a smile.

"For my honesty, today is shit. All around shit. Just shit. Shitty shit," she said.

I started giggling as this was a line she got from Bradley. I looked at my son and saw a grin start to creep across his face; he knew Hailey had a plan.

"Yeah Mom. This is a shit day!" he chimed in.

Hailey continued, laying out her plan of action.

"Here is the deal. We get McDonald's: two burgers each, large fries plus ice cream 'cause Dad just died, and we are sad. Really shit sad," she said while waving her finger back and forth. I was laughing now and was about to say something when she cut me off. "I am not done! We also get to sleep in your bed because Dad isn't here anymore. You have to share with us now!" she demanded.

"Yeah, Mom. Sharing is caring," my son added.

I started to laugh so hard at these two kids of mine when a flashback hit me. Hours ago, I'd been crying so hard, I thought I would never laugh again. I thought I would never again have that feeling where you laughed so hard, it hurt. Now, with my two kids telling me how things were going to be from now on, I was laughing harder than ever. It hadn't yet been months or weeks after Bradley's death; it hadn't even been a day. I was laughing within hours and by my side was my next best everything—my best friends. I started laughing even harder when I realized this as I took their picture by the river. They were building a plan together to get McDonald's, not crying over Dad.

That night, with both babies in my bed, I hoped I would find peace in sleep. I don't remember falling asleep. I do, however, remember being woken up. Something startled me in my sleep and my heart felt like it had burst open. The best way to describe the feeling was that it was as if a defibrillator had been pressed against my heart and it shocked me right out of bed. My heart was pounding so hard. It was unbelievably heavy and with a strong, sharp, racing pulse. It felt like my heart was going to come out of my chest. This is what woke me. There was no sound. Complete silence surrounded me. I grabbed my chest and placed a hand over my heart. Tears started to trickle down my face as I knew it was Bradley. I *knew* it was him. I also knew something had happened with his heart. I said the words, loud and clear, "Go back to sleep!" and it was as if someone had shot me in the ass with a tranquilizer. I immediately fell back asleep. Lights out.

The next morning, I was in a daze. My sister was on her way from Vancouver Island. My cousin stayed by my side until my mother could tend to me. I couldn't stop thinking about what I'd experienced and felt the previous night. I was afraid to tell anyone. I feared I would be told I was crazy and would be carried off to the Psych ward. In truth, I didn't know if I really believed it myself.

I crawled into a hot bath; I had made it hotter than ever. I don't remember thinking about a single thing in that moment. I just curled up in the running water and stared blankly at nothing, my eyes swollen, red, and puffy. I felt like life itself had ended for me. There was nothing left for me to bear. Then I felt a cold, little touch of life on my face. It pulled me towards the light of her face. Her bright, blue eyes pulled me forward while her two little hands cupped my face. It was the same way Bradley had drawn me into him. The sun reflected off her freckles and a golden glow shone around her light, brown hair.

"Everything is going to be ok, Mom." They were a daughter's soft words. She caught my tears in a little glass bottle with one hand still on my face. "Daddy deserves every single drop!" she said.

I cried so hard, astonished by this child. Her strength in the face of her mother's suffering amazed me. She was happy that I cried so much because I filled up her little bottle. The smile on her face turned my tears of sorrow into joy. She locked my tears inside that bottle. Months later, I found out Hailey had put glass beads that looked like diamonds and little rocks she had polished herself inside the bottle too. My little girl, what a wonder.

My sister tucked the kids into bed and put me to bed as well. Once again, sleep came quickly, but I woke up suddenly to a loud banging sound. I noticed my son had crawled into bed with me and was amazed he didn't wake up because of the noise. It was so loud. I looked outside, convinced someone was trying to break in somewhere. This thumping sound came in sets of two beats. I counted seven sets. Then, there was a brief pause. I looked out the window more intently. No one was out there. Everything was in place and still. The sound came back louder than before—stronger and more pronounced. This time there were only three sets. Then, it stopped. I wasn't scared at all. I slowly sat up and moved to the edge of my bed. No one heard this? How could that be? It was so loud! Then, once again, I fell back asleep.

The next morning, I made it my mission to find out what the fuck had made that sound. I described it to my sister and asked her if she'd heard it. She'd heard nothing. I asked the kids. Still nothing. I ran outside in my pyjamas and slippers and began banging on every neighbour's door, asking if anyone had heard the sound. I was frantic. The sight of me scared my neighbours. They were all taken aback by this tattooed, slipper-wearing, bleary-eyed, blotchy-faced woman with purple hair who looked like she was on drugs. I must have seemed like a crazy person. As if that wasn't enough, when every single person said they had heard nothing, I lost it. I went to the alley behind my house and started hitting anything I could with a two by four, trying to re-create the sound I had heard. I had no luck, and with this sound imprinted in my memory, I returned home and slumped down on the front steps.

My sister came outside with a cup of tea and placed it down beside me. I was embarrassed. I wished just one person had heard what I had heard the night before. I wiped the tears from my eyes in defeat. I looked up at my sister who was near the edge of the deck. I was honestly waiting for her to tell me (in the most loving way possible) that this was normal, that grief has a way of stressing our bodies and minds to the point where we can't tell real from make believe, and at times our minds make up stuff. Instead, she said something I will never forget. Something that made me promise myself I'd never take for granted my truth, ever again.

"Sweetie, I think what you heard was meant just for you!"

Now I really cried. She believed me. All this time she'd never doubted what I heard, felt, or experienced. I am usually considered the strong one in the family—maybe it's because I am the oldest—but my sister was the strongest person I had ever known on that day when she shared her light with me with those words. I think she knew where that sound had come from, and she knew who had sent it. But I didn't fully understand until later in the summer when I was sharing the story one sunny afternoon with my father.

"Do you think it sounded like a heartbeat?" he asked.

"Yes, Dad! Dad, it *was* a heartbeat!" I gasped.

I knew it was the truth the minute he said the words. My whole body tingled. He and I discussed it further, as we love talking about spiritual things. We decided the seven sets I'd heard were the seven spirits, and the three sets symbolized new life. Bradley did pass on Easter Monday after all. "And on the third day he rose again." On the third evening after he passed, I was lying on my left side, facing the bathroom. I opened my eyes slowly, just ever so slightly. The light from the moon was cascading from the bathroom window into the bedroom. I saw a silhouette move towards me from the closet. It looked like a man, but it had no distinct features. A transparent shape was before me, almost like a blur. I laid still, eyes half open and I smiled. I smiled because I felt Bradley's presence. I fell back asleep.

I was so grateful for these gifts: the beating heart and seeing Bradley one last time. All my senses were charged and armed with the truth of everything I believed and followed. I felt I'd been promised that my beliefs would never be doubted. I'd been promised I would never be alone. I had been promised that eternal life exists after we die. My faith had given me hope like never before— unquestioned and unwavering hope, all due to faith. I could believe in something unseen. Faith is like the wind: I can't see it, but I feel its wonder. I hear the sound of life the wind brings. All its beauty is due to love, and I have loved deeply. And because I am loved, I am no longer lonely.

I never actually got to say goodbye to Bradley. I never got to feel his breath or hold his warm body in my arms one last time. But I shared something with his father that was almost the same. I remember the shame I felt as I struggled to face him. "I tried to save him. I am so sorry. I am so very sorry!" I kept repeating these words to him, and, for the first time, I saw that man break down and cry. We cried together; I buried my face in his chest, as my tears soaked his jacket. The same sounds of mourning echoed from both of us. It was then that I felt I held Bradley again. His father's essence was identical to Bradley's. I closed my eyes as I heard his words.

"It's ok. This is not your fault," he said.

It was all Bradley—every single bit of it. Holding his father tightly in my arms, I got to say my goodbye.

I have experienced many injustices in life.
I still hold anger for some that were done. On the surface
it may appear that I harbour malice. Something is changing
that; deep in my heart I hold only love for those who hurt me.
I can forgive those who damaged me.

(From Bradley's journal, February 2021)

TEN

On the fourth day after Bradley's passing, the chief coroner called. I was so numb by this point. All I knew for sure was that I needed to hear what the coroner had to say. I needed an unbiased professional to tell me the reasons behind a very young man's death. Most importantly, I needed to know if my fears about his health had been wrong; I needed to know if all this time, I had been a bat-shit crazy, controlling, and obsessed wife who had suffocated a good and healthy man. I swore I would listen to every word and would accept what the coroner identified as the cause—but deep down, I just knew it had something to do with his heart.

"Bradley's heart was three times the normal size," the coroner stated.

"What is your diagnosis for that?" I asked.

"Malnutrition," he replied.

He explained to me how unusual this was in someone as young as Bradley was. It would have taken years for a heart to get as big as his was at the time of his death. The coroner said that further into the autopsy, it became clear why his heart was so stressed and big.

"Once I examined his liver, I saw that it was very enlarged and fatty," he said.

"What would have caused that?" I asked.

"Alcohol," the coroner replied.

I will never forget how I felt when he answered. After all those years of trying to warn Bradley and his family, I finally got confirmation that I had been right all along!

A l c o h o l.

In my mind, the word sounded out in slow motion, in an odd, warped way. My heart started pounding, and I felt dazed. I had to ask him to repeat what he'd just said to make sure I had heard it right. Before I hung up the phone, I shared Bradley's history with the coroner. He validated everything I said and expressed how justified I had been in my attempts to change this man's habits. His findings proved my suspicions, and the evidence was clear. A toxicology report was recommended and months later I found out the immediate cause of death: mixed drug toxicity; the second contributing factor: cardiomegaly (an enlarged heart); the classification of death: accidental.

Bradley died at thirty-two years of age due to an accidental overdose. The partners in crime that caused his heart to fail? Fentanyl and alcohol.

Toxicology analysis revealed fentanyl and alcohol; both cause respiratory depression and decreased blood oxygen levels that can result in death. Autopsy findings included an enlarged heart (cardiomegaly) with thickening of the left ventricle of the heart, which increases the risk for lethal cardiac dysrhythmia and sudden death.

– Chief Coroner, Coroners Act, S.B.C 2007 c.15 S. 16, S 69

To put it simply, Bradley's blood essentially poisoned his heart and it stopped. His decision to casually have some drinks was the catalyst to slow down his very weak and inflamed heart one last time. Bradley was a ticking time bomb. His liver was failing him, which is why yellow puss-like fluid had been leaking out of his belly button and his skin had turned a yellow hue. These are all symptoms of liver failure, also know as fatty liver disease. The smell I took in months ago and that lingered about was his body rotting from the inside out.

I never asked Bradley why he drank. I knew why he did. Instead, every so often, I would ask him, "Why are you in pain?" The illness explained why Bradley was in constant pain, why his legs were swollen and restless, and why he had gained so much weight. I believe it was because of Bradley's long struggle with pain that alcohol wasn't enough that night. As I had witnessed so many times before, he reached for something stronger to numb his state of mind: illegal drugs. Though there was no evidence of this that day I found him, the toxicology report identified the culprit: fentanyl.

Bradley hadn't been getting any sleep, nor had he decreased the stress in his life. I am not a doctor, but I am the biggest geek around when it comes to fitness and nutrition. I'd studied everything there was to know about this man's health: his habits, actions, and moods. There was so much evidence that his lifestyle was sabotaging his well-being. His eating habits were so destructive. His body was infected by a disease that took away any chance of a healthy lifestyle. After doing some digging and research of my own, I gained a more in-depth understanding of what I believe happened to Bradley's body and state of mind.

Cytokine, a protein that fights inflammation in the body, is only produced during sleep. Due to a lack of sleep, Bradley's body wasn't producing cytokine, which led to a weaker immune system. I also read that caffeinated and alcoholic beverages increase depression. Not only was Bradley fatigued, he also was suffering from an organ dysfunction. In this situation, the body will try to protect itself and compensate by pumping excess blood to the damaged organ. This often leads to unexplained weakness, confusion, impaired judgement, and severe energy loss. The pathophysiology of liver-related fatigue presents additional symptoms that compound over time. Depression and anxiety may be worsened by changes in the body including an inability to produce serotonin, an important mood regulator. Serotonin production can cease completely with fatty liver disease. Bradley was always fucking moody. He was so moody, I had different nicknames depending on what mood he was in: was it Gollum or Eeyore? Sometimes I would get both, as Bradley bounced back and forth between them in the course of a single day. Nothing was enough on those days—he was so irritable. He'd stay in the dark on a sunny day, with the windows shut. Everything was too much for him, and his tasks were left unfinished. He just had no motivation at any point during the day. I saw his state of mind deteriorating with the pain and trauma he'd experienced. It attacked him the most while his body was weak. He was no longer making any healthy changes to his lifestyle. He had stopped writing in his journal, doing his schoolwork, or eating the meals I made for him. All of it disappeared out of his life. He would actively isolate himself. Personal hygiene became a chore and was no longer a priority. His energy was something dark to be around. His spirit and light were inactive.

Everything came together for me when I was given the autopsy results. It was like the missing piece to the puzzle; all I'd seen, for all those years, came together. His liver played a huge factor in the weight gain. This damaged his confidence in his identity as a man and his self-esteem was nonexistent. The liver problems made it impossible for his body to digest food and absorb nutrients, which ultimately led to malnutrition and heart failure.

Healthline.com[1] reports that:
> A chronically poor diet with a sustained intake of fatty, sugary, and/or salty foods is one of the root causes of fatty liver disease. With lifestyle factors such as excessive alcohol, this can be the leading main factor of liver problems.

I was curious as to why the coroner said alcohol was the cause of the fat build up in Bradley's liver. Doubting that it was solely due to poor diet, I called him back months later while doing my research for this book. He informed me that they can determine the difference between food fats and other fats associated with alcohol consumption. In Bradley's case, he indicated it was clear that alcohol was the cause. Knowledge is power.

"See fuck face? I was right this whole time!" I said out loud, looking up to make sure he'd hear me.

Linda: 7; Bradley: 4.

I smiled and giggled softly to myself. I could just hear him reply, "It's not a competition, Linda!"

Linda: 7; Bradley: 5.

---

1   https://www.healthline.com/health/fatty-liver

I know with all my heart Bradley had wanted to quit. He wrote about it often. He wanted all the pain to end. He wanted to be rid of alcohol. I believe Bradley knew his body was slowing down. He was the smartest man I have ever known. His immune system was compromised, he was barely sleeping, his body was inflamed, and stress was eating away at him constantly; his heart bore all the weight of that. I know now, more than ever, that alcohol was partly to blame. It was the kindling to the fire. His body was quitting on him.

In the three years leading up to Bradley's death, I searched for information about mental and physical health. In 2019, I focused on myself and worked on minimizing my stress. I opened up my heart, and also created the boundaries of self-love and self-care. I concentrated on perseverance and forgiveness—forgiveness for the errors committed by others and, most importantly, those I had made myself. Then in 2020, I expanded my knowledge. With my heart in the right place, it was time to exercise my mind. I wanted to connect both my heart and mind. I practiced yoga and meditation; it was a form of self-preservation. I bowed my head to my heart and allowed this to be my true self. I knew I needed help in 2021. My heart and mind were in place, and now it was time for the final step: I needed to train my body. I hired a nutritionist. She taught me that emotions are the most important ingredient when it comes to our overall health. She taught me to incorporate exercise, movement, and proper nutrition into my lifestyle. Balance was key. I became clean, lean, and honestly, a beautiful, healthy machine. My heart, mind, and body were now all in sync—they worked as one. When all three connected in love, I found my spirit. I was kind. Gentle.

Many people get it wrong. You shouldn't exercise your body first. You need to exercise your heart by freeing it and allowing it to love openly. Then, exercise your mind so your thinking will change. Lastly, exercise your body. Heart, mind, and body—only in that order.

I'd led by example, hoping Bradley would pull through. Instead, I watched him deteriorate before my eyes and there was nothing I could do. I continuously asked for strength throughout 2021. I heard that word: *gentle*. At first, I made an honest mistake and assumed it meant I should be gentle to him. How naive I was. I came to realize, after Bradley's passing, that it was meant for me. I was being told to be gentle to myself.

Fear is the beginning of wisdom. Love is what breaks you. Once you take accountability for your actions, you will be redirected to understand what true love is. It is a hope that perseveres even in the hardest of times. Love needs to be broken into us, every day. Bradley lost all hope in his career, his schooling, his home, his family, his health, and himself. With no hope, there is no peace, and life is not worth living. Bradley wouldn't forgive himself, therefore he felt no love. No number of distractions could silence those voices in his head, the voices of his demons, full of venom and lies. He doubted himself; he doubted his worthiness. This was the most powerful lie. He tried to release the guilt he held on to through drinking. His alcoholism tricked him into feeling a temporary sense of freedom from his pain. It numbed him, this silent killer. It didn't matter how much I loved Bradley; he didn't see it. Not that he couldn't have seen it with a simple attitude adjustment. He chose not to. He didn't love himself enough.

I often caught Bradley saying, "You can't hurt me. I am unhurtable." Bradley had to deal with the truth of his pain in order to heal. Without that truth, he would never heal. What was his truth? I think he felt dead in the world, and he felt dead inside.

He was beyond feeling, beyond emotion, and beyond hope. This was the inescapable road that Bradley travelled deep down in his heart. This was the biggest truth of all. Bradley never wept. He wasn't able to find a place where he could. His silence is what killed him. He suffered in silence. Silence took away his spirit. The alcohol scarred his body. The pain corrupted his mind. His suffering stopped his heart from ever accepting true love. His brokenness left him questioning his worth. Bradley once wrote in his journal, "I am broken and can't be whole anymore."

A hardened heart won't forgive. Bradley's heart wouldn't accept love, whether it was self-love or love from anyone else. He once warned me, "I'm beyond help; don't give your heart to me." Bradley died because of his suffering, which I think for some people can be addictive as well. He dwelled on his suffering. He got stuck in it. He wallowed in it, never gaining its benefits to achieve a higher perspective.

Despite my attempts to confront him about his problem, despite the tears I shed over it, he would not change. After ten years, I had nothing more to say. I had said and done it all. I had outgrown the abuse and disease. They finally got old, and fast. I was ready to level up and walk away, knowing that I truly did love him, but that I loved myself more. I had resolved from that moment on, I was going to live my life more fully and more abundantly.

I had never seen Bradley scared, but I believe he was afraid of letting go. He kept hanging on to things, above all the pain. On reflection, I think his drinking was the only coping strategy he'd ever known—and he couldn't let go of it. This was his attachment—not love. Bradley hung on to the idea of love because he was so good at giving a false representation of it. His love had so many conditions, and that kind of love left him empty.

Love should be unconditional. Bradley wouldn't receive love and the true meaning behind it. Therefore, he was back to where he started in the cycle of pain. He abused his body, and the wrath invoked by his pain was the by-product. Before Bradley ever abused me, he abused himself, every single day. This was his disease. This was his illness.

To understand what I have written is to know love. Real love. Tough love. Unconditional love. True and perfect love. I had to lose Bradley because it was my grief in the wake of his loss that allowed me to finally come to understand this: the best thing to happen to me was Bradley's death.

Too many times we neglect family to stay in our "normal life." We sometimes avoid going to see family because of past trespasses, judgements, or anticipations of what the gathering would be like. Therefore, we actively avoid one another.

(From Bradley's journal, December 2019)

ELEVEN

I confined myself to the house. Still in shock, I would stare out the window and see nothing. I heard nothing. I couldn't speak and the smallest sound had me on the edge of screaming. I could not stop crying. All I saw on repeat in my mind was Bradley, cold and dead on the floor—blue veins, shaved head. How I missed his curly long locks.

I didn't realize it, but I didn't eat for days. My sister was by my side, trying to feed me half a banana, encouraging me by eating half herself. I held on to the only piece of Bradley I had left: the necklace I gave him with his engagement band and three cross pendants. Each cross represented one of us: my son, my daughter, and me. I wrapped the necklace around my hand, embracing it as if it was him. I wouldn't let it go. Like a child I clung to it. I remember how bright the sun shone through the windows. I was too afraid to leave—to leave my home, to leave his home, to leave him. My mother, who was also with me, saw all this happening and said something that I still replay in my head every day.

"Sweetie, he isn't coming back. It is safe to go."

She was encouraging me to be brave, but I broke down and cried in her arms, wailing over and over for my beloved—my Bradley, my everything.

"Go!" she demanded, holding her tears back as best as she could. I needed her courage to walk out the door. She knew how much I loved the sun and how much I loved walking. Before long, I reached a baseball park. I sat down on the bench and looked into the clouds. How strangely familiar this felt as my hands touched the wooden bench. I sensed the same smell of freshly cut green grass. I closed my eyes.

"Him!"

I heard the same word I had heard that first time I saw Bradley on a baseball field. The sun broke through the clouds and for the first time in what felt like forever, I felt the warmth. My skin came back to life. My tears sparkled in the sunlight. I saw so much light. The presence of light and warmth gave me hope. I stood in the sunlight at last; it was only a matter of being willing to come into it and believe in a power greater than me. I realized I had never been alone, nor would I ever be. Closing my eyes, I could feel myself getting lighter, as if I was floating towards the clouds. I could sense Bradley, and I knew he was safe. He was warm. He was light itself. All of a sudden, I started laughing so hard. I was remembering his answer when I'd asked him years ago what would happen if he died before me.

"I will haunt the shit outta you!" he had replied.

At the time, I had been so angry at him for not taking my feelings seriously; but now, the fact that it had come true had me laughing. I hated him for leaving me behind, but I was grateful that he had taught me to always laugh, no matter how bad or ugly the situation was. I would often try to pout, but he would have none of it. He'd grab my knee and start tickling me and teasing me, calling me a sucky baby, or saying, "Oh Linda!"

Linda: 7; Bradley: 6.

I wanted to stay in this moment, but there was work to do. I had to make the funeral arrangements for Bradley. Even now, I remember the feeling of sitting in the funeral home like it was yesterday. Everyone was annoyingly soft spoken—too soft. What I wouldn't have given for a loud swear word in that moment. The tiptoes of soft, controlled movements were the only sound. Here I was, the weight of the world on my shoulders, my face mask covered in tears and snot. I wore all black. I recognized I looked too young to be in this situation, so I figured this would make it obvious that I was the one in mourning. I made sure my sweatpants were not covered in dog hair.

The best part about the funeral home was that it was just outside my door—not even a block away. I was shown into their conference room where I looked at the options for urns. My mind churned over all the different styles of containers they had to hold a person's remains. I was thankful Bradley wanted to be cremated as the coffins were expensive as fuck. I couldn't believe a wooden box that would be covered in dirt could cost that much. What happened to slapping some plywood together and calling it a day? Or we could build one of those wooden funeral biers, place coins on his eyes, and light a torch. Wiener roast anyone? I starting to laugh as I thought about how Bradley would have acted if our places had been reversed. He'd be making jokes and getting a laugh out of the situation, no matter how horrible it was.

I was handed the paperwork, which broke down the costs

of his cremation; I was shocked at how much it cost to bury someone. I considered keeping his remains in a plastic bin; I knew at some point down the road we would be spreading his ashes anyway. But then I thought of his mother, and I was flooded with feelings of guilt. The last thing I wanted was her thinking that I placed her precious son in a cheap plastic box. The thought made me laugh out loud, and I'm sure the saleslady thought I was losing my mind. Why the fuck does it matter? It might be a cheap, plastic box, but it's not a reflection of Bradley's worth; it's just a receptacle for his last physical remains.

The next topic on the agenda was discussing a public viewing. Thoughts of how I had last seen him overpowered me. I explained to the funeral director that I didn't want his family to see him in that state, and nor would Bradley. She said they could recreate his appearance when he was alive and began to go over how well they could conceal any flaws. When she started talking about all the chemicals and makeup, I interrupted her and bluntly said, "No. There will be no viewing." It broke my heart that his friends and family wouldn't get to see him, but I just could not do it. I *would not* do it.

The next day, I met with Bradley's father, mother, and brother. Sitting at the kitchen table, I informed them of my decision. My whole body was shaking. I was so broken-hearted that they would not get to see him again. I knew it was for the best, but I also knew the family were not happy with my decision. Nevertheless, I focused on what I believed was right and my strength got me through it. The family requested three things on Bradley's behalf: the first was that he stay together; the second was that he stay with me; the third was that I take all the time I needed. I looked down at my hands and then lifted my head slowly. It was time to reveal Bradley's autopsy report. I always knew in my heart the truth, but now I placed it before his parents and brother. I felt sick to my stomach. I will never forget the silence that followed. It was like someone pushed the pause button on the remote. Everyone at the table looked down. Tears were running down my face, but I felt like a burden had been lifted. The truth had been revealed, and I no longer had a secret to keep. I felt free—relieved.

"Are you at rest now?" I heard one of them ask.

I stared down at my hands without replying; but with all my heart, I said to myself, "Not yet!"

It's hard to believe you are gone. I've endured a tragedy and all the pain that comes with it. Can this pain still grant me perseverance? I have to acknowledge the truth in order to grow from this deep pain. I need to heal. Healing opens the door to one's heart, a true sign of love. That love is our power. My dedication to self-care and self-love—this is the compassion I must reach for inside my broken heart. I keep looking for you. Everywhere. I wake up to what I believe is you: your smell and warmth. I keep listening for the sound of the dishes being washed. I imagine wrapping my arms around you, breathing you in, and matching our heartbeats as one. I hold on to crumbs of you. I found some of your hair caught in your old hairbrush—an old brush you must have used before we shaved all your curls off. I held on to it. I haven't had a single dream of you since your death, but in the daytime, you're always before me. I daydream more than ever. I am so tired, and I sleep so much. I don't want to waste away. I gave all I am to you. Now, there is nowhere to go. What is my purpose now? Without you I am no one. You were my everything. Why do I deserve the silence? I am a basket case, but this won't surprise you. You don't need me anymore. I need space to mourn after you. I am lost. It hurts so much, my love. It hurts. I can't breathe. I don't want to have to go through this. Is this what I was created for? I want to disappear. My colour is fading. The sun is still shining but it feels like it's half the size. I want to be where you are in the stars. What happened to growing old together? How could you leave me? I feel alone. Will I ever be discovered?

I wrote these words in my journal on April 16, 2021. I didn't know it then, but I was in the first stage of grief: denial. I needed to feel something, something close to real. I hadn't experienced physical intimacy for so long, I longed for that release. I got in my car and drove slowly. I was in such a fragile state, I was scared I might crash. I pulled up to the store. I was humiliated and my sorrow overwhelmed me. I remember picking something out that was in a bright package—my eyes were drawn to it. The saleswoman never stopped talking. I found her high-pitched voice annoying. It was like nails on a chalkboard. As I was paying for my item, she took my purchase out of the box to show it to me. "You have got to be fucking kidding me," I thought to myself.

"Don't you have any other colour besides black?" I inquired.

"No, unfortunately not," she responded, hesitating before placing it back into the box.

Tearing up, I asked, "Can I have the pink display one instead?"

"No, I'm sorry; that one is for display only," she answered, seeing the look of despair on my face.

With tears running down my face and with red swollen eyes,

I sniffled and handed her my credit card. The clerk witnessed my display of emotion and glanced at her co-worker with a sympathetic look.

"We can always place an order for the colour you're requesting. It may take two to three weeks ..."

"No, I will take it. Fucking been long enough!" I snapped, cutting her off. I grabbed my purchase, drove home, and went straight to bed. I held this long, black toy in my hand, feeling the silicone between my fingers. I was still crying as I felt more alone now than ever. Memories of past rejections replayed in my mind. How often had my womanhood been pushed aside and my beauty wasted. In the midst of my pain and self-pity, I started to giggle. Out loud I shouted, "I shall name him! His name shall be ... Dillion!" Dillion already came charged and ready to commence his duty.

"Part of our customer service is to make sure you get the full experience as soon as possible with our guaranteed convenience," the women back at the store made sure to tell me.

Picturing the worried look on their faces as I was crying about the colour back at the sex shop, I burst out laughing hysterically at my pathetic self. It was fucking convenient, alright? I fucked the shit out of Dillion all night. I had to charge the poor guy by morning. The best part? I purchased Dillion with money my brother gave me. He was so generous to his sister, helping with any of her needs.

"Anything you need, just ask!" he said, as he gave me money.

Ha! Thanks bro! Bradley was right: I should have made a mold of his dick. He always told me it would make a great souvenir.

Linda: 7; Bradley: 7.

Shortly after I wrote the journal entry, and after this experience in the sex shop, I reached out to a trauma counsellor. I was desperate to share my story. I needed to take my blinders off and let the light in. I needed to follow my own advice—the same advice I had given Bradley for years: ask for help—and most importantly, ask for the right kind of help. I wanted an explanation for my pain. I wanted to understand what was happening to me. I decided after my first session, it was time for *me*. I walked away from all obligations. I called all my clients and let them know I was taking a leave of absence. I didn't know how long I would need, and I honestly didn't care. I figured this was the one time I could walk away from everything without any guilt.

The only reason I *could* walk away from everything was because my family helped me financially. My brother, my father, and my kids' father didn't hesitate. I can't find the words to describe the love I was given. A dear client and friend started a Go Fund Me page on behalf of me and the children. Within seventy-two hours, it had raised $6,200.00. Friends of Bradley's mother, who had known him as a boy, gave us gift cards, money, and food. I had never met any of these beautiful people. More and more people showed up at my door. Flowers were constantly being delivered, and the house smelled so fresh. They all said that this is what Bradley would have wanted: his family looked after. Together, my clients and the church community fed us for months. The school Bradley was attending lowered their flags in his honour and his classmates gave a beautiful speech about all he was to them and the community of the Bachelor of Education program. I will remember every card, word, post, and message of love sent. The prayers lifted me up, recharging me for the next day.

When my sister took her leave, I had a girlfriend stay with

me. She focused on rehabilitating my energy for the tasks at hand. She spent time with me, helping me to become aware of my surroundings. She guided me on what needed to be attended to immediately. She helped create space and peace within my home. The first item on the agenda: the three dogs. The dogs continued to be an issue and I finally had to take a stand. It wasn't their fault, but I resented these fuckers. They were Bradley's responsibility, and he had never taken care of them properly. I was always so exhausted. I worked, I ran the home, I took care of the kids and, in the little spare time I had, I squeezed in my own extracurricular activities. It was a battle to find time for myself and exercise. These dogs were not properly trained and were running amok in the house. My girlfriend said something I will never forget. "You're the alpha now!"

Honestly, I would have adopted two of the dogs out right then and there if it wasn't for my son's feelings. I just wasn't up to the task of dealing with them, but my son's words penetrated my heart; I had lost my shit one day after cleaning up dog puke. I had a full plate already and this sent me over the edge. I was screaming and having a full-on mental breakdown in front of my kids, when I overheard my own words: "I'm fucking done. I can't do this. They have to go!" I yelled, bent over, cleaning the puke and shit off the couch. Both children were staring at me in tears. My son was holding a towel to his lip, which he'd cut while roughhousing. With bloody lips and what was the greatest display of courage I have to admit I had ever seen, he addressed me in a deep, direct, and strong tone.

"Mom, stop!"

You have to understand that for these kids, when Mom was mad, it was the scariest thing ever. The dragon was out! But he grabbed my Bible, turned to a specific page, and told me to read out loud, reminding me I must listen to him as he was the man of the house now. So, I read. Out loud.

"Do not worry . . ."

When I finished, he spoke to me carefully, as tears streamed down his face. "You see Mom? Do not worry. We have lost so much already, and I know this is hard and the dogs are going to piss you off a lot. Together we can do this. If you get rid of the dogs, you will regret it."

To my amazement and shock his words were bang on. The teenager before me put me in my place. He took his broken-down, mentally exhausted mother and lifted her up just enough. The top priority with these animals was to bring back order. My father always said when we were children that we didn't obey him because of love; it was actually due to fear. Out of fear, we grew to respect and love his authority. Now I had to bring order by instilling fear. What better way to do this than by cutting off the youngest testes! My God, can you imagine if we could take every man who wronged us women to court and request to have their balls hacked off? Off with their balls! Fuck, am I a good time.

The second priority? I needed to stop treating the dogs like babies and establish some boundaries as the new bitch in town. These untamed animals were out of control and did whatever they pleased in my home. I never had a leg to stand on as Bradley always made excuses for them. This was my house now, and I was not spending another waking minute cleaning up after undisciplined fur babies. The female, Astin, had awful anxiety and attacked the other dogs the minute a sound startled her, or something didn't go her way. She still pissed inside which drove me nuts—not on my new floors! Bradley and I had argued the most over her. She was always the problem and instigated every fight. Her anxiety affected all of us. I repeatedly suggested she should be given to someone who could provide the space and attention she needed, but Bradley refused to listen. He put her on medication instead—an $80 a month prescription for a hormone imbalance, or some shit like that. It was bullshit! She just needed discipline and consistent routines. She needed a safe space to keep her anxiety down, so I started putting her in a kennel at night and separating her from the other dogs at mealtime. It was like a miracle! This simple change did the trick as dogs won't urinate where they sleep. No more pissing in my home! I took her to the vet who confirmed the pills weren't needed anymore. As a woman who had experienced living in a stressful environment, I empathized. It's no wonder that sometimes women seem crazy! You can suck it, Bradley! I was right again!

Linda: 8; Bradley: 7.

I promised myself I would give it one year before making any permanent decision about the dogs' futures. The end of the year came like a crack of thunder in a storm. While we had some success with Astin, the dogs were still too much for us and I ended up putting Astin and Altas up for adoption; they deserved better homes and a more suitable lifestyle where their needs would be met. I made all the changes I could possibly think of before coming to this heart-breaking decision. No one else in the family wanted to put in the work and attention the dogs needed, and it was too much for me to do on my own. I knew it was the right thing to do, but I still struggled to find peace after they were gone.

A year later, my daughter and I were on a walk and had stopped to look for agates under a bridge when Hailey yelled,

"Mom! Look! It's Astin!" She leapt for joy as she started to make her way to the dog and the elderly couple with her. I quickly grabbed my daughter's shoulder and told her to look at me as tears formed in my eyes.

"Sweetie, you're right! That *is* Astin, but she is no longer our dog. We don't even know if that is her name anymore and we need to respect . . ." I started.

Hailey cut me off, cupping my face in her hands. "Mom, she is our dog and always will be. We must go to her," she said. Hailey knew I struggled with guilt over letting the dogs go. Deep down I couldn't refuse her. She knew that I needed this more than anything.

"Excuse me. May I pet your dog?" Hailey asked politely.

The lady gently refused, mentioning Astin's high anxiety. I was struck by this woman's attention to Astin's needs. I had worried about her the most because it would take a special someone to love her and give her the protection she needed. I was wearing a hat and knew the woman didn't recognize me. I took the hat off slowly. "Is the dog's name Astin?" I asked.

Astin's ears perked up when she heard my voice. The woman recognized me, and my purple hair, immediately. She approached me with her husband and Astin. I stifled my desire to grab Astin right away, hold her, and ask for her forgiveness, and instead began chatting to the couple. Meanwhile, Astin covered my daughter in kisses. I couldn't believe it, but Astin knew who Hailey was. Could that really be possible?

"She looks so beautiful and happy. Thank you so much for taking really good care of her and loving her. Do you mind if I say hello?" I asked, trying to hold back my tears.

I bent down slowly and carefully placed my hand out to Astin in case she was shy or hesitant. Astin jumped up on her back legs, put her front paws on my chest, and pushed her face into my neck, kissing me endlessly. I broke into tears and Astin's licks swept them away. I was so happy in this moment because this beautiful animal showed me there was nothing to forgive. She was grateful for her new life. And she still loved me.

I found out from the couple that she loved herding the cats on their farm in the country. This made me laugh so hard as I knew how much she loved to run and play tag with my children. I could tell that the husband adored her and that he cuddled next to her every night.

"She has to be in the middle between us," the woman told me.

Finally, I had peace. To think, my daughter and I were supposed to leave that spot an hour earlier but Hailey insisted we stay a little longer. We almost missed them.

Altas was still a pup when he was adopted by another woman. His personality also needed someone special—someone who would be goofy and fun like he was. His character matched the young woman who called about him. Months after she had brought him to his new home, she called and thanked me for such a wonderful gift. She said anytime I wanted to see him, we could meet at the dog park. Her favourite thing about him was his nickname, Moose. She laughed as she now understood why I gave him that nickname. He was heavy set and was so awkward when he walked or ran. He'd slam into doors and corners, or he'd run full speed into the couch. After just a single pat, he would push his head into you and collapse on you, continuing to push his head harder into your body while making the funniest sounds. I never understood where his behaviour came from until I came across a video of Altas when he was a puppy. Bradley was holding him up, tucking him into his face, and making sounds in his ear. I like to think Bradley imprinted his character onto his fur babies.

Ayms became our family dog. His behaviour and health improved once the other two were gone. He was finally happy and free of stress. I realized I wasn't the only one who had been struggling with the presence of the other two dogs. I call Ayms my kitty; he is so content and well trained, he acts more like a cat than a dog. He sleeps most of the day, is super quiet, and loves being chased. I see so much of Bradley's humour and temperament in this dog. He can be a spiteful little bugger when he doesn't get his way; however, no matter where I am in the house, if Ayms hears me cry, he comes to me every single time. He sleeps by my feet on the floor and cuddles up to the children. Ayms has become a magnificent dog, and I love him like he's my own child.

I am so grateful for the gifts of strength and endurance so I may lift up others who are not as strong as myself. I know in my heart of hearts I do this with pure love and not to please myself.

(From Bradley's journal, November 2019)

TWELVE

Spring had arrived and summer was approaching fast. I had lost one of the great loves in my life, but there was another one on the horizon, waiting to be grabbed: baseball—the one activity Bradley always supported me in. The very thought of stepping onto a baseball field without him made me sick. I cried every time I tried to picture myself on the diamond. Baseball was the only thing that I felt kept Bradley's attention wholeheartedly on me. He knew my game and how I played. Often, he would come to push me and coach the other women on my fast pitch team. The girls loved his energy. He was an amazing coach and was super knowledgeable about the game. These are some of my favourite memories—watching someone I loved show such passion for a game I also loved. He shared all he knew. It was powerful.

Anytime I was complimented on my fielding skills, I would laugh. If only they knew the drill Bradley would make me do for hours on end to learn how to read the ball before it was hit. He would tell me to lie face down on the ground, like I was about to do a push up, while he got ready to hit the ball from home plate. During the warm-up, right before he hit the ball, he'd call,

"Ready up!" I would pounce onto the balls of my feet and try to find the ball. After a few rounds of warm-up, he would make me lay down the same way, but there would be no "Ready up!" warning. I had to listen for the crack of the bat hitting the ball and move my fucking ass. This was all because I said I hated being an outfielder. For years, I played catcher in fast pitch and first bag in slow pitch. After playing those positions, my mechanics were off, and I figured I just couldn't be an outfielder anymore. Bradley wouldn't have it.

I grew up learning to bat and infield by watching my cousin. He is such a talented and beautiful player. The best part? He is so humble; he shows no arrogance, whatsoever. I admire that the most—that and his love of Superman. I always looked up to him and my uncle on the baseball field. My father taught me to watch the ball, and to never be afraid of it. To this day, he calls out his nickname for me, Tig, just before I swing. If I miss, he'll say, "Watch the ball, kiddo." That always gets me smiling and reminds me of our bond together.

With the guidance and example provided by all four of these men, I became quite a player in both fast and slow pitch. As a female player, it is nice to know you can play most positions comfortably and, most of all, with confidence. However, one of these men was now missing. In my eyes, he was the most important part—the key. How was I ever going to step onto that field again?

I love the game. I love the sun and being outside. I love the smell of freshly cut grass and the sound the ball makes when it hits a glove. I love the atmosphere and the people it brings together: the baseball family. In the months leading up to the first baseball season after Bradley's death, I lost sight of all this in my grief. Bradley wasn't here to see me, or to come home to after a game. The pain of this closed my heart, and I wanted nothing more to do with baseball. I would try to envision myself stepping up to the plate, but I kept hearing the words "I can't." Fear struck me down as I felt all my skills and talent leaving me. It was just like you see in the movies, except this wasn't a movie. This was real, and this was happening to me.

One day in late May, I received a Facebook message from a woman, an acquaintance from when I used to play. It was a kind and simple message. "Would you be interested in joining me to watch the men's fast pitch tonight?" I love playing baseball, but I also love watching it—especially men's baseball. Everything is so much faster and sharper. It was nice to be asked by someone who was basically a stranger at the time to join her for a game. It also crossed my mind that watching baseball during my struggle with grief might help me gain the courage I needed to start playing again one day. Although, if I'm being completely honest, that wasn't the only reason. Men in baseball pants? Drool! Nothing is sexier! That was a fantasy of mine: fucking a guy in ball gear. Needless to say, I jumped at the invitation; I even stayed to watch the late game, too.

Eventually, I had the courage to step onto the baseball field to actually play a game and try to remember the joy I had once known. The beginning of the first game was rough though, and I started to shake. My heart was pounding, and I felt light-headed. I felt like I could hardly breathe, as if I was drowning. Tears started to come in waves. I stopped before the plate and hung the bat on my shoulders. Everything went silent. I was dreaming. This had to be a dream, like the ones where I am naked, and everyone is staring at me. I felt a flush of cold on my forehead and realized I had pressed my head against the metal of the back catcher fence. I couldn't see well, my eyesight was blurred from the salty tears and sweat. I looked into the crowd—searching, hoping to hear his voice just once more. How I needed him the most in this moment. This was not a dream. This was now. I stood against the fence and started coming back to reality. I backed away from all the players waiting for me to take my stand in the batter's box. Then, I heard a friendly voice speak on my behalf to the rest of the players who were getting impatient.

"She just needs a minute."

I rushed to gather myself quickly. My two children were watching their mother attempting to find whatever courage she had left to play a game she loved. I was trying to focus on what Bradley would say to me at that moment.

"Where are you?"

I knew the answer. My heart was there but my mind wasn't able to connect. I closed my eyes tighter, hoping I would be able to concentrate.

"Where are you?!" This time, it was sweeter, and yet louder and more powerful. I felt a wind of breath on me. I flashed my eyes open. There we were, face to face; I was on one side of the fence and he was on the other. His eyes were bright and sharp. He looked into me, not down on me. It was my son.

"Answer me, Mom! Where are you?"

Still shaking and crying even harder, I answered, "I am here!"

"Then what are you waiting for?" he questioned. My daughter ran over to join my son. The two little humans I created stared at me from the other side of the fence. With their smiles giving me hope, I approached the plate with tear-stained cheeks and pulled my hat down with shaking hands. I dug my feet into the earth, taking a long deep breath in. I readied my bat. Before the pitch was released, I heard my son shout out as loudly as he could, "Nobody loves you!"

A roar of laughter came from the field, from the players and everyone else within ear shot. I couldn't stop myself from falling to my knees and grabbing my stomach as I felt the good pain of hard laughter.

"Come on, Linda. Everyone is waiting on you!" chirped my daughter.

My kids were like two peas in a pod. I didn't strike out once that whole game. I've learned to look for their faces now, to listen for their voices, and to rely on the most important truth of all: they have always been my biggest fans. Baseball was even better than I remembered, especially playing with them by my side, our hearts connected as one. The essence of Bradley was in them.

Having baseball back in my life was a help, but I still felt like death on a cracker. I was pale. My skin was flaky and as dry as sand. I still had holes that needed to be filled with hope, drive, and passion again. I just couldn't get there. Instead, I distracted myself by putting work back into my home. Fresh coats of paint, storage clean out, new flooring—I went crazy, pushing myself non-stop for more. I guess you could say I wanted to make something mine. I wanted order and to be rid of my old life. It was time for something new. During all of the renovation work, I had time to reflect on what was missing in my life. My lack of energy and the constant strain of stress left me weak and tired. Standing back, I realized I had done more in the two months since Bradley's passing than I had in the decade we were together. I really needed to catch up on my life and the one place I knew I had to start was in my own home. One's home should be a haven. It should be somewhere one feels safe, loved, and welcomed. It should be a place where you can sit back in utter joy over a sense of accomplishment. The degree a person invests in their lifestyle is shown by how they manage their home. I finally needed this more than anything. Having lost so much, I knew I couldn't bear losing this.

No matter how much renovation work was going on, I started my day with a walk. Most days, it was an hour; some days, it was longer. Sometimes, I would find a quiet place to sit, allowing my dry skin to soak up the sun. I fell in love with the light and the warmth of the sun on my face. When I walked, I allowed the pain to come and for nature to heal me as I took in the true beauty before me—the sound of birds chirping and fresh water running downstream. It was cleansing and restorative. The sun reflected off the water with such a remarkable and breath-taking radiation. It was like a beam of hope. It felt like a weight was lifted off my shoulders. After I came back from my walks, I was lighter.

One particular day, I kept walking. My body must have known what was coming. Earlier, I'd received a phone call from the funeral home. Bradley's remains were ready to be collected. Writing these words, I still feel like this is all make believe, just a dream—a very bad dream. I can feel the weight of what was left of him in my arms to this very day. I walked to the funeral home and couldn't hold myself together. I couldn't escape what was really happening. They placed Bradley in my hands. He was in a plastic box that was no bigger than a shoe box. I have never felt anything so heavy in my life. I started to hyperventilate and couldn't speak. I asked to leave. I walked as quickly as I could to my gate, barely breathing and wailing all the way home. Once inside my yard, I collapsed in the dirt. I cried out in agony. I made sounds I'd never heard before. It was an anguish so deep that I felt torn apart. All of me was broken. I lay on the cool dirt in the fetal position, wrapping my arms around Bradley. I became completely still. I couldn't move.

I woke up to stars and the cold of the night setting in; Bradley was still in my arms. I slowly rolled over onto my back and looked up into the blue-black sky. The moon and the stars shone down on me.

"Time to let go!" a voice said.

I knew I had to take my hand off the box. Bradley would have wanted me to live—to really live, and to stop holding back. He would always be with me wherever I went; however, if my hand remained on this box, I would be stuck in the abyss of pain and trapped forever. With God and Bradley as my only witnesses, I declared, "Now you know more than ever how much I love you." I slowly lifted my hand from him. I started singing a song to him—something that held us together in that moment. I fell asleep in a pile of dog shit. It was smeared across my face. Even in death, Bradley kept his sense of humour!

Linda: 8; Bradley: 8.

The children and I had a jade green urn custom made for Bradley's remains. My daughter knew he loved rocks and gem-stones as much as she did, and my son knew green was Bradley's favourite color. Tanner picked out a verse that we had engraved on it. I found myself repeating this verse often to grant me com-fort and peace. Fatherhood was what these two children gave Bradley. In his heart, they were never anything less than his own children. Bradley wrote once in a journal entry how he'd always wanted to be a father. Fatherhood was a gift to him; in it, his purpose was fulfilled. We decided as a family to place Bradley's ashes into his urn together.

I did my very best to prepare the kids' hearts for this task. I wanted to keep an open mind, but I also wanted to protect them.

It is not every day you bury a family member and put your hand on his remains. The thought terrified me. Was I a bad mother for asking if they wanted to participate?

We were all standing at the kitchen table, looking down at Bradley. My daughter's eyes were as big as coconuts, and my son was looking for my reaction, anticipating tears at any moment. We didn't know what to expect. We had never seen the ashes of someone's body before. As I opened the plastic box to transfer the ashes into the urn, my daughter broke the silence.

"Mom!? You think we will find Dad's eyeball in there?" she asked, with an excited look on her face. I was shocked, but she was seriously looking for his eyeball. I laughed and was trying to explain to her how cremation worked, when my son cut me off. He encouraged his sister.

"Yeah, Hays. I bet we will find his leg in there!"

"Tanner!" I gasped in shock.

Both of them were laughing now and peeking into the bin. I opened the bag inside the box and gave the children scoops to carefully pick up Bradley's remains and place them in a new bag that was in the urn. Hailey looked at the scoop and shot me a doubtful look. She placed it down abruptly, and just dove her little hands into Bradley. Tanner took this display in and followed her lead.

"Dad wouldn't want us to be sucky babies about this," Hailey said as she ran her dad's ashes through her hands, building a mountain of his remains. She actually giggled. This was not what I had expected, nor prepared for at all. I looked at Tanner. He kept digging and sifting through the ashes.

"Tanner?" I asked softly, worried that he wasn't doing well at all. "What are you doing?"

"I am looking for his damn leg!" he smirked, looking into my eyes. He was keeping up with his sister's sense of humour. He was always good at playing along to please her. I started to relax and sat back, allowing both of the children to play in their father's remains. I may be judged as a mother for this lack of respect in handling Bradley, but if you saw the display of true love from my children that I did, you would have done the same. The memory this moment created was important, and I know Bradley would have loved every minute of it. He gave the children the gift of expression, an honest and open way to share with others simply. He always told them, never change who you are, even when others don't take the time to understand you. I took this as a sign and watched in joy.

We took turns filling the urn, and then we sealed it. It was then that I saw little tears form in their eyes. We all gathered at the head of the table and wrapped our arms around one another, proud of the difficult thing we had achieved—and proud of the fact that we had faced it together.

My son saw me panic as I noticed the top of the urn was scratched. I ran around frantically trying to find something to polish the marks off. No luck! I started to cry. I was so disappointed in myself. I hadn't had Bradley's urn in my possession for an hour and it was already fucking scratched. My son placed his hand on my shoulder. I sobbed away, telling him how I had wanted everything to be perfect.

"I know Mom, and because you didn't make it perfect, you're going to hell for this one. Dad is watching and he is very disappointed in you," he said with the biggest smile on his face, handing me a tissue.

I burst out laughing. I grabbed him and gave him the biggest hug of his life. His words hit home that day. He taught me to stop putting so much energy into emotions like this. He was right. It was such bullshit and a waste of my time. Why should I bother to remove the scratches? They showed the most important truth of all: something can be imperfect and still be beautiful. This was a lesson I needed to prepare me for what lay ahead.

I struggle daily with the desires of the flesh. These struggles consume all my energy. I am so tired of being subject to the past and future. Living in the past and always focused on the future destroys any peace, contentment, growth, and awareness in the present moment.

(From Bradley's journal, May 2020)

THIRTEEN

Halfway into the summer, I was going through the second stage of grief: anger. I was angry about everything—the paperwork, lawyer fees, dealing with Bradley's estate. I was angry with the family and their demands over Bradley's possessions. Some demanded his ashes to be spread in one place; others wanted them to be spread in a different place. Many were angry at my decision to not allow a viewing at the funeral. Others wanted his death explained and the autopsy results revealed. I was, however, mostly angry with Bradley.

I would love to be able to say that our time together had always been loving and healthy, but if you've read this far, you know it wasn't like that. It had often been the exact opposite— a kind of hell. I didn't need to take half a year off to mourn his loss. I had already planned and had prepared to live without him when I had decided to leave the relationship. I had already let him go. The half a year I took off was to mourn me, to mourn the pain inflicted on me by someone who was very sick. In order for me to mourn effectively, I had to get angry.

I had lost so much staying with this man. He cost me my

health, relationships, money, career, family, and more. His disease traumatized me; it destroyed everything good in me and everything good for me. For ten years, I had been trapped in his secrets and his lies. I hadn't been living for myself; I was living for him. I was being drained. I was constantly showing up for him and giving him all that he wanted while I ignored what I needed: his love and his acceptance of me. At one point, I had wanted to end my life, convinced I was the problem. After his death, those thoughts ended immediately; however, I wasn't able to express my pain and anger came out when I was triggered. I was told by my therapist to prepare for this and not to distract myself. I needed to make the day meaningful, even when it was hard. For far too long I had placed walls up and over my heart, which was stopping me from living. It was time to face the pain.

One of the biggest and most painful triggers for me was when people, whether it was friends or family members, would express how kind and loving Bradley had been to them. They would talk about how he had taken so much time to be compassionate with them. They described how they had been struggling and feeling overwhelmed, and Bradley hadn't let them stay there. He had made them laugh and had pulled them out of their funk.

"*Wonderful*," I thought, sarcastically. Learning about this had been like torture for me while he was alive. When he passed away, it hurt me so much more. I fucking hated hearing about it, but I put a fake smile on and tried not to scream. He gave whatever good he had to these people, but behind closed doors he pissed all over me. This explains why I almost believed I was the problem and wanted to kill myself. I had spent years helping him to recover and cleaning him up. I had stayed with all the puke, shit, piss, and sometimes even blood. I had attended to his weakened mind, heart, and body. All the while he kept kicking me while I was down. I was his only love, his only light of hope on Earth to lead him to a better path. Despite his mistreatment of me, I still believed in him and deemed him worthy of so much more. But please share with me how beautiful he was to all of you, how he gave you his best while he took a shit on me. Did you know he'd come home from entertaining you, giving you a great time, only to yell, curse, and release his wrath on me? When many assumed I was controlling or withdrawing from family or crowds, it was actually that I was a victim every day of my life with this man. There were so many times I was subjected to a complete mess when he was drunk; he'd pour his bottles of liquor out onto the floor, swearing to me that it wasn't a problem. *I* was the problem. The venom of his words cut deep into my soul. I'll never forget when he told me, "You're a controlling cunt. I drink to numb myself and get away from you. *You* make me drink more; you're a life-sucking, fucking whore."

I joined a group through the local hospice to help me deal with these feelings. They had a ten-week program that guided you through the stages of grief. Five weeks into the program it was "Remember Your Spouse" day—like a show and tell. Another gentleman—who had lost his wife to cancer—and I were selected to make our presentations on the same day. I wanted to skip this event. I felt sick to my stomach. I was not even close to being ready to present how I felt about Bradley. I was still struggling with the pain of recent events, and I had not come to terms with the trauma.

As I watched this man set up his laptop, while I held a single framed 5x7 picture of Bradley, I kept thinking, "Fuck. I should have gone first." This guy had made a slideshow with a smorgasbord of beautifully edited photos of his wife—*with timed music!*

Fucking prick and his fancy fucking computer skills. Who does that?! I can understand doing it for a celebration of life but at grief counselling? Damn! I guess when you're retired, you have a lot of time on your hands. This slideshow lasted an hour—*a fucking hour!* I kept sinking lower and lower in my chair the whole time. I was gripping Bradley's picture so hard I broke a corner of the frame. Once the slideshow was finally done, I was asked to talk about my spouse.

"Oh, good." I said in a harsh and spiteful tone.

I slammed Bradley's photo on the table and sat there with my eyes closed. I was in front of all these people. I was vulnerable, and I was *angry*. Across from me sat the retired guy, with his computer and his soft music. "Ugh!" I thought. But I knew I could do this, and I could do it without any bullshit. I had promised myself I wouldn't lie anymore.

Before I opened my eyes, I heard that soft, gentle voice once again. It said, "Tell your story."

So, I did. I was raw, blunt, and honest. I told them that this photo was the only one I had of Bradley when he was sober. I told them I hated that he had left me here to deal with all this on my own. But I also told them how I was glad he had passed as I could no longer be hurt by him. I had been set free and a burden had been lifted off my shoulders. I explained to them that if he had just listened to what I had been telling him all these years, he would still be alive. He could have accomplished so much but nope! The fucker was dead and in an urn in our house—a house that I had turned back into a home where I was left to face a future without him.

No one moved or said a word. I felt so ashamed for what had come out of my mouth. I wanted to run for the door. People who know me well know that after I get really angry and let out all the emotional vomit, I cry. I am by far the ugliest crier, too. I stood there with my head down in guilt and tears streaming down my face; the room became completely silent. Once again, I was being stared at and no one dared make a sound. I knew I was the one that had to break the silence. A devilish smile came across my face through the tears.

"So, obviously we all know what stage of the grief cycle I am in!"

A roar of laughter came from the crowd; even the instructors, who were supposed to stay as neutral as possible, couldn't keep a straight face. I looked up at the slideshow guy. "Fuck you and your PowerPoint presentation!" I snapped. People started laughing even more. "Seriously though, can I hire you for when I have a celebration of his life?" I asked. Now I was laughing too.

"Won't be much of a slideshow with only one photo," he replied.

Fuck, did we laugh. I haven't laughed so hard in my life. Everyone thanked me. I was the youngest member by twenty years at least. Each and every one of these people were just as raw and broken, yet they were holding me up. I tried to apologize for my behaviour, and they shut it down. They said it had been the best thing for them. They appreciated my honesty and that I told the ugly truth about the healing process. Who would have guessed? My behaviour actually made an impression—my thumbprint left behind. Isn't that the truth in the world today? Men are taught not to shed tears or to express emotion, so they can appear strong. Women are told it's not proper or classy to share their opinions, let alone express their anger. These were the cultural expectations the other people in that room had been born into. They were all from the baby-boom generation. I had expressed openly and honestly what they had been feeling all along—and they appreciated me for it. My crazy purple hair, my skin covered in tattoos, my trucker mouth, and my angry bird temper had given them all a new perspective.

When the pain in someone's life is so deep and so unbearably painful, anger will come, every single time. When you cannot run from it any longer, anger appears and then produces tears. The stronger the pain, the stronger the anger—and the stronger the tears will flow. Tears authorize us to experience an alternate reality where we can see things we didn't see before. They allow us to feel things deeply—more deeply than we've ever felt before. Tears shatter indifference.

What none of them knew is the very minute I got in my Jeep, I broke down into a mess. I cried and cried and cried for what seemed like a lifetime. I finally cried all those tears of pain. I allowed myself to be free and, on that day, I truly forgave Bradley and everything he did to me. I forgave him for all the injustice and for all his indifference. I didn't need him alive to say sorry; nor did I need to spend any more time wasting away from the pain due to the past. I let it all go, all because I chose to shed tears that shattered my indifference towards him.

July 14, 2021

I've got some good news and some bad news. The bad news is I'm never going to be the same; there is a part of me that will never be whole ever again. I lost this part of me, and I can't ever replace it or get it back.

The good news is I have started to accept that, and I allow myself to suffer. I allow myself to think and remember all the good and the love that was given. I remember the joy I knew.

The morning after my performance at the hospice, I wrote these words in my journal. I had realized in my darkest moments of anger that I couldn't steer away from the pain. I realized if I tried to avoid it, I would stay in pain, and rob myself of any joy. So, I decided to confront the pain and to feel it.

The truth was, Bradley had no love for himself. I realized I had been selfish to ask a very ill man for something he couldn't give. Bradley had believed he was unlovable. How did I know this? Because he never shed a tear. This was his indifference. I had asked a broken, sick man, who believed he was unlovable, to love me. It didn't matter how many times I cried, how hard I worked to support his dreams, how many gyms I joined, or how many sexy outfits I wore. I still went to bed every night going over every single detail wondering what I had done wrong, how I might have misunderstood, or how in the hell for that brief moment I could have thought happiness was a possibility. I had given him everything he had ever wanted: a home, fur babies, children, education, money, a career, and me. At times, I believed if I just put my head down and worked harder to provide for him, that my example would convince him to see the light in me and he would start showing up for himself. I thought he would give us a chance to succeed, together. I thought together we could build a lifestyle of endlessly giving to one another. I hoped he would get healthy and strong and take care of me like he did so many others. I hoped that he would finally walk through that open door. But he never did.

Seeing Bradley suffer for years wore me down. He honestly became such a burden to me. Someone who is so sick for so long and doesn't improve no matter what you do for him, makes you feel worthless. I was depressed, suppressed, and divided. And yet, I never stopped believing we could forget the past and rebuild.

Now I know what a woman in love does. She remembers the vow to stay in sickness and in health, for richer or for poorer, until death parts you. I had made the decision to leave, but I never actually left. I stayed with him not because I forgot, but because I forgave him. I wanted Bradley to be free from his anguish, and I had been willing to let him go to find his freedom. I figured if he came back to me, then I'd know he had been mine to begin with, and he would be mine forever. In the end, he didn't come back to me, and I learned that he had never been mine to begin with.

After all I had endured, with his death upon me, I had to start again. I had to make another life without him. Little pieces of my soul were finally coming back. Pain, with time, turns into little pokes. Years of my life had been taken from me and I felt at times like it was all a waste. Did I not deserve the happily ever after part? I had wanted that for us. Still today, I can't believe he is gone. I find myself asking, "Is he really gone? My Bradley . . . gone?!"

All this will eventually fade and only love will remain. I meet new people every day. Most of them were always there, but to me they are new. I had never looked up before now. They give love gorgeously and openly. There are no more secrets, lies, or abuse. I feel safe now—safe to be what I always dreamed I could be. He can't hurt me anymore. Most importantly, he can't hurt himself.

Now, anytime I play back the most excruciating and devastating events in my mind, I see how much he had to have been hurting to inflict such pain on someone else. We both have been set free. A burden has been lifted. A life has been reborn. A weight is gone, and relief has been given—not because of his death, but because he is no longer suffering. Now do you understand the last sentence I wrote in chapter ten? The best thing to happen to me was his death because it was also the best thing for him. He once wrote in his journal, "I struggle with desires of the flesh . . ." Bradley's daily struggle was to try to escape the man he was ashamed of. Bradley, consumed by his shame, destroyed any possibility for peace and contentment with life. All his energy was taken up by the narcissistic character traits stemming from the disease. The manipulation left him tired as he constantly worked to convince others of his lies. Gaslighting created an illusion for his future. Bradley suffered as a result of his past more than anyone else ever did. "I am so tired of being subject to the past and future," he wrote. There was no growth; he could never get there. He lived a false life—a continuous fantasy—because he chose to hide his pain. He chose to live a lie. Bradley met a force he couldn't destroy, so he destroyed himself instead.

The love I have for him prevails. I've placed my ego aside so he can rest in peace. A family member told me once that I knew him best and that they would follow my lead because of all I knew of Bradley. I can say with confidence that this is what he wanted most: to no longer be in pain. As much as I hurt because of his passing, knowing his suffering has ended is a comfort. My old ways of thinking had to die, too, in order for me to accept that there is no love without truth and there is no life without death. I had such an intense love, which I know now is a precious possession greater than life itself. It is also one that comes at a great cost.

*I pray for the strength to live my life in moderation and
continue to rebuild the foundation of my life: supernatural
rest, abundant love, and humility.*

(From Bradley's journal, January 2021)

FOURTEEN

In the weeks and months after Bradley's death, I felt all eyes on
me, staring and watching my every move. I was bombarded with
annoying questions by everyone around me. "I am fine" was all
I could muster. My blank eyes looked beyond them. I couldn't
hear the whispers, but I could feel them. To the outside world,
my mind was on autopilot; I was numb and dazed. But inside
my mind and heart, I replayed every good memory of him, over
and over in hopes I would not lose him. I tried to remember
everything: his breath on me just before he kissed me; his smell,
laughter, and heartbeat. His deeply passionate eyes were life itself as they looked upon me. He was such a beautiful kisser, and
he knew how I loved his kisses. He would grab my face in his
hands, making me feel so tiny as he pulled me near him. I would
run my fingers through his long curly hair as I held on to him.
We would stay there for as long as it took. It was the connection
of two souls in one another's arms. We would hold our heads
together, our foreheads touching, as our arms embraced. Eyes
closed, together, we would breathe one another in deeply. Inhal-
ing each other's essence, energy, and smell. Together we would

breathe a single breath—in and out. I would feel every inch of him, and he would feel me—all of me. In the good times, we came together this way, often and naturally, almost like we just knew to do it. We came in unity, surrendering who we were.

In those early days of grief, I doubted everything I did—and everything I didn't do. My mind was in another dimension, floating far and away from reality. Day to day choices seemed lost in translation. Most times I would just disappear into myself. I wouldn't remember if I'd brushed my hair or put deodorant on. I had to rely on others to gently feed me, bathe me, and at times, make me smile. Some understood but most didn't. Those who didn't took advantage of me. I was exposed, a vulnerable creature. I felt sedated in space and time. The weight of uncertainty consumed me. I found myself drifting between past and future, unable to find the present. Unknown shadows discovered my light. Fear kept me hidden, alone, in the dark. My bones felt heavy, my soul felt rotten, and my poor heart ached. The world, as I knew it, kept spinning faster and faster. I couldn't catch my breath; dizziness consumed me, and I would fall over in a faint. A storm emerged without any warning, without any sign. I never saw it coming. The whirlwind of darkness uprooted my present and cascaded into my future. What future? A collision of disruption and despair was all I could see. My plans were buried in the chaos. Losing him had been the hardest thing I had ever had to live through. Even though I had decided to leave, I wasn't ready to say goodbye. I wasn't ready to let him leave. What I would have given for one more day. Just one more second. I was fully exposed for the world to see. Every crack in my skin exposed my vulnerability. Everyone saw my spirit taken out from under me.

I lived life like a recluse. It was a solitary life, avoiding others at all costs. I couldn't stand to have another person tell me,

"Everyone grieves differently," or "Give it time."

The worst was someone forcing a hug onto me. Like, fuck right off. Man, I hated to be touched and hugs were the worst. I was in the longest stage of the grief process: depression. The only thing I felt somewhat safe to do was to get out of the house and go grocery shopping. Or so I thought. One day, I was on a regular shopping trip, just like any other day. I grabbed coffee, cream, etc. I was walking down the snack aisle when I froze, realizing I had just picked up a bag of Bradley's favourite. I looked at my cart and realized everything I had picked up had been for him. My muscle memory had taken over my mind. I started to hyper-ventilate and threw myself down on the floor, clutching the bag, screaming, and crying all at once. A young clerk and a security guard approached cautiously. I can only imagine what was going on in their heads. I hadn't bathed properly in weeks and my hair was a tangled mess. I had blotchy eyes and puffy skin. I was wear-ing my favourite nightshirt—which was so worn it was thread-bare and covered in holes—half tucked into my paint-splattered sweatpants. There I was, sitting down, rocking back and forth in the middle of the aisle. I must have looked like I had es-caped from the Psych ward. The only thing missing was a hos-pital bracelet.

I opened my eyes to a pair of black shoes. I had forgotten where I was and slowly picked myself up, wiping my snot from my face with my sleeve. I was vibrating in shock when suddenly, I heard *pop!* The bag exploded and little orange puffs flew every-where: in my hair, in my face, on the floor, in the cart, and all over the shelves. I started to cry even harder, apologizing as I tried to pick them up one at a time. At this point, a crowd had gath-ered to take in the scene. I was rushing now, trying to grab them all and shove them back into my cart, my pockets, anywhere I could. Bawling, I fell to my knees again, half hanging on to my cart and half dumping all the snacks I had just gathered back onto the floor.

I laugh as I write this, picturing the poor men's faces who must have thought I was high on drugs or something. The funniest part to all of this? I was mortified and, in my attempts to be chill and calm collecting all the mess I had made, I remember one distinct thing: *crunch, crunch, crunch!* That was the sound of a bunch of people stepping on those orange puffs while trying to help a grieving widow. At least they cared more about me than those damned things. When I got home, my kids looked at me and started asking, "Where the food at?" and "What is that orange stuff in your hair?"

"Next time you guys can do the shopping, 'cause I fucking quit!" I yelled, as I slammed the bathroom door and finally, after weeks, took a bath.

I swore I would never walk into that store again; however, I am no fucking coward! I still march in there proudly, and every now and again the security guard recognizes me, and we share a little laugh.

"We stocked up on your favourite snacks today!" he tells me, with a smile.

"Go fuck yourself, Fred!" I reply.

We both laugh at each other, and I walk away, although I give him the finger every time.

My six-month leave was coming to an end. I was terrified of the cold. The warmth of the sun kept me going all summer long. I am naturally more active in the spring and summer months when I eat cleaner foods. I knew winter was coming, and I recognized what that meant and the battles that lay ahead. I wasn't afraid of finding a routine again; in fact, I craved it. Things were going to be very different, not like before. I planned on changing everything, from the way I worked to how I ran my home and organized my lifestyle. The thing I was petrified of was the thing I knew I could no longer hide from: writing. I had the summer to distract me, but I knew full well that I would be called to attention come the fall. There was no ignoring it or escaping the truth.

I tried to use my depression as an excuse not to write. Many times, I wanted to walk into the doctor's office and ask for medication. I wanted to get drugged up and numb myself all winter long. I wanted to feel nothing and deal with nothing, but that very thought made it all worse. I was actively seeking out ways to avoid thinking about my trauma without realizing that I was delaying the healing process. I was set straight by someone who helped me find myself again and put me on the road to discovery. This person, who I'll call "Mr. Blunt," pulled me out of my depressive state through an act of courage. It was a reaction—a spark—that started a new chapter in my life. It was really something quite small, but it was so powerful because it was right, and this person spoke up before anyone else.

Our conversation started with me explaining why I wouldn't cut men's hair anymore. My last memory of cutting a man's hair was that awful incident with Bradley. His was the last man's hair I had touched, and it was a horrible experience that left me scarred. It broke me, and I remained broken, unable to revisit the event to repair the damages.

"You mentioned that you were not going to give men's haircuts anymore. Not that you have to say why, but I am here to listen," Mr. Blunt said.

I took his words as a sign to open up and talk. So, I said, "I am really talented behind the chair, especially with a pair of clippers. I enjoyed my conversations with men. They kept me honest and at times, slapped a little reality into me. I always felt like I left something with them, but they gave me more in return. The bonus was a great haircut . . ." I paused and felt goosebumps developing on my arms. My hands were shaking, and sweat was forming on me like there was a sudden heat wave.

My throat tightened but I continued, "For some reason, I never made Bradley happy with my work. I couldn't talk to him like all the other men. I wasn't able to make a difference—not just with his hair. I could never make an impact with my words. He always questioned everything—from my skills as a barber to my wisdom. I never felt good enough to cut his hair or to talk to him and I would work harder than ever to try to reach him." By now the tears had come. I wanted to stop but I had to continue. As my heart pounded in my chest, I resumed. "The truth is, I felt accepted and loved by all these other men. I felt heard by them. Conversation is an art, a beautiful dialogue. More than anything, I wanted this so badly with Bradley. I felt guilty because I distracted myself to fill in a gap, a hole inside of me. I would share my stories and the great conversations I had with my male clients, in hopes that he would want a great haircut and conversation, too." I took a deep breath, preparing myself for what I was going to say next, out loud.

"Bradley surprised me one afternoon by asking me to give him a haircut. I was overcome with joy. I had high hopes that he finally wanted to be a part of something that was so important to me. Unfortunately, he did the exact opposite. He punished me by making me shave his head; it was something he knew would bring me pain, and he tortured me through the whole process. There was no conversation. I had no opportunity to show my skills. He knew he could have easily done the work himself, but instead he made me shave off all his long, beautiful curls. I finished in tears and walked away crying. He attacked me with his words, saying this was why he never let me cut his hair."

I paused for what seemed like a lifetime. I was trying to be brave, telling this stranger my story, but my shirt sleeves were wet from wiping so many tears away. Then, the silence was broken.

"It's a shame that you are giving up on such talent!" he said.

That's all he said. I was left speechless. My mind was racing over those words. Where the fuck was the pity? "Feel sorry for me, you son of a bitch," I thought. "I have a very good reason to walk away from all this." But Mr. Blunt wouldn't have it. He put me in my place and was quick to force me into submission. The truth flooded my mind and this individual's words penetrated me deeply. The minute I got defensive, I knew that what had been said was right. I just hadn't been ready to hear it. "Mother fucker!" I screamed out loud while sitting in the barber chair the next day. I was staring at a box full of my barbering tools labeled "For sale."

"It's a shame that you are giving up on such talent!" Those words changed everything. Why couldn't this person have been normal and just said what I wanted to hear? Come on! Didn't I deserve to be pitied in this situation? I sat in that barber chair all day staring into the mirror, trying to find any excuse to fire back at this person and his words. Suddenly, I began laughing. I realized I had wasted all this time and energy fighting against what needed to happen. Because of my stubbornness and refusal to take responsibility for anything, I was blaming Bradley for all of it, and this person called me on it. It must have taken a lot of courage for Mr. Blunt to listen to my sad story and say the difficult, but true, thing. Many would have just condoned my decision to walk away for good.

But instead, I had been called out on my shit. I realized that not only was this person right, but their words were *powerful!* No number of tears on my part took away from what had been said. I really hated that, which made me laugh. My sad, sappy story hadn't convinced Mr. Blunt one bit. Damn it! I really figured I deserved nothing but endless sympathy. Just shaving Bradley's head had devasted me and, on top of that, Bradley had passed away! Was that enough for this person to let me give up? Nope, not even close.

Before long, my talent was restored. Great conversations replaced bad ones, and one painful memory was softened all because someone took a chance on me and listened with intent. They took the opportunity to teach me something important: never give up, no matter what. I also learned that words have meaning when you are ready to listen. I continue to look up to this person and allow their influence to inspire me.

After this, a chain reaction commenced. Everything started to fall into place, beginning with this book. Words started to materialize on the page and chapter after chapter appeared. I went back to working at my salon, and I was booked up for months. I started to repair my important relationships. Others, I let go. I saw what was possible for me and sought it out with efficiency and precision. Money was no longer an issue. I made goals and plans to follow through. I felt a new sense of freedom and self-worth. More than anything else, I was determined to stay the course. There would be no more distractions and no more pity parties. Many who in the summer had promised to be there for me, disappeared once winter arrived. I wasn't surprised, nor did I lose sleep over it.

Holy chicken biscuits was I on *fire!* I looked fine as hell. I had found a gym and was working hard on getting into shape. My body was toned, with defined abs and I was starting to get that apple booty I had been daydreaming about for years. I was no longer wearing clothes that hid my figure. I was constantly meeting wonderful new people. Strangers would come up to me and tell me how beautiful I was and that I was glowing. I still cried, but I also sometimes laughed until it hurt. I wore less makeup, sang louder, and skinny dipped regularly. I fell in love every day. I learned to love the silence, I looked up more, and I smiled often. I danced naked in the morning, took myself out on dates, and used tattoos to transform my body into a work of art. With every new tattoo, I felt more of my story being told. I took pictures of myself—sometimes while I was naked. I made mistakes, often.

I taught myself my new favourite word of all time: "No."

I will say it again, "No."

One more time: "No!"

I even made a song out of it. It's called "No, No, No, No!"

At first, the family got the polite version: "No, thank you." Soon after, as some took everything I did or didn't do, personally, I went back to the original: "No!" I stopped caring what others thought and said about me. Those words became powerless and no longer had an effect on my life. It was important for me to accept what the universe gave me, and to decide if something served me and my purpose or not.

The feeling of insignificance, weakness, and lack of control conflicts continually with man's ego, pride, vanity, and identity. Shed these ideals. Open your heart for your thinking must change.

(From Bradley's journal, June 2020)

FIFTEEN

I had never really understood what a relationship was until I chose to have one with myself. I felt at times this fact was why I allowed the abuse to go on and for Bradley to continue to take from me. I was so desperate to be loved, held, and adored that I was left feeling weak; I had forgotten my worth and that is why I accepted the abuse. At times, I doubted if Bradley ever loved me. I struggled back and forth in this thought, questioning the way he treated me. Why would someone be so hurtful if they loved you? I started to doubt myself. Was I making all the pain up in my head?

Cleaning was a great distraction from my endless questioning of my self-worth. One day, I was downstairs in Bradley's old study moving boxes around to make room—my son was going to use the room as his bedroom. I was about to rip down this tacky green sheet of fabric that Bradley had stapled to the wall when something made me stop. I found myself gazing at this representation of a tree. I remember Bradley seeing it in the mall years ago; without a thought, he had gone into the store and bought it. This was unusual for him. I asked him why he made such an impulsive purchase, but he never answered me. It was as if he couldn't give me the answer, like he didn't understand it himself. I never did find out why he bought it, but he insisted on putting this huge green tree—it was almost seven feet tall—on the wall. It had an infinity design on it, and I caught myself staring at the repeating lines and circles. It was a never-ending flow, but of what? There was a bed of leaves scattered on the ground near the roots of the tree. To my surprise though, there were no distinct branches; it was almost as if they had been torn off.

I felt as if this tree was me.

I realized that, just like this tree, I have gone through many seasons. As I looked at it, I began to imagine that the leaves might represent the many people who come and go in a person's life. The wind blows one direction, and the leaves fall to the ground and rot away. So many people have appeared and then disappeared from my life, but I will never forget the lessons these leaves tried to teach me. The branches of a tree might appear strong and sturdy, but they can break and leave permanent scars. I felt the moment I stood up for myself out of a sense of self-worth or made changes based on my own values and morals, some of my branches broke. It hurt, leaving me exposed and weak. Some branches hit me on the way down, smacking me in the face. Then I thought about the roots at the base of the tree— at its very heart. A tree cannot survive without its roots. There are more leaves than there are branches and more branches than roots; but the roots are the most important. Your roots will always show you the importance of holding on to what grounds you.

A dear friend and soulmate once said to me, "People will be forgotten when they were only meant for a season in your life." The acquaintances in my life are leaves on my tree—people I only know casually. In fact, they are people I know very little about. At times, I see these people on the baseball field. I have played with many of them since my youth. With baseball, it has never been about winning for me. I would rather lose a game and treat others with respect, than win and treat others poorly. This has sometimes put me at odds with a few leaves. I love the game, but because I love people more, some of these leaves have dropped from my life.

Unfortunately, after Bradley's death, it became clear that some members of his family were just leaves on my tree. I thought some of them would really be there for me, but they weren't. I was devastated by the actions carried out by some of his family, and, sadly, in the end I wasn't just grieving the loss of Bradley but of many of his family members as well.

They fought with me over Bradley's ashes and what would become of them. The choices I made regarding his remains should have been respected, but these people went against my wishes and did what was best for them. I can respect that but not at the cost of taking from me, his partner, and from his children—and most of all, taking away from Bradley; however, it was made very clear to me that only Bradley's blood family would be allowed to spread his ashes.

I needed more time and money for the celebration of life I wanted to plan, but they wanted to be in charge of organizing it and left me out of the entire process. I felt not only cast out and ignored, but also harassed. I felt pushed and pulled in every direction as I attempted to respond to what others wanted. In the end, I made promises to Bradley's family in response to requests that never should have been asked of me. I handed over his ashes and let them take control of the celebration of his life so that I would be left alone and for the fighting to stop. I wanted my life—and my children's lives—back.

They continued to demand answers about how Bradley passed, exclaiming, "We deserve and have a right to know!" They all wanted to know why it had happened. Why hadn't I reached out sooner to let them know that he had gotten so bad again? Their tone was accusatory. "You must have said 'no' to him. Now he is dead!" I think on some level, they took their anger and sorrow out on me thinking that might bring them closure. But I was also heartbroken. I couldn't help myself, let alone anyone else, to understand what had happened.

While this was unfolding, I looked to my father for support and as always, he was there for me. I was constantly on the phone to him in tears. I couldn't believe this was all happening to me. I questioned everything that I had done. I was Bradley's partner. Didn't I deserve his family's respect and love? Feeling defeated, I told my father, "I have to try to make them love me, so they all understand who I was to him."

My father, who very rarely raises his voice, brought me to attention. "No! Elisha, no!" he yelled. "This has nothing to do with you. Are you listening to me?" His voice was angry, and I felt my knees shake. "You cannot make anyone love you. That isn't love. You cannot make the blind see."

A little over a year after Bradley's passing, I received a message from a member of his family. It was another request for pictures of him and me, the dogs, the kids, etc. It had been over a year since I had heard from any of them. No one had checked in to see how we were doing. There had been no contact. I denied the request, and it wasn't because I felt hurt by their lack of contact or rejected because they had left me out of the planning for the celebration of Bradley's life that they were going to hold. It was because I had already given them the one photograph that I had taken of him. I didn't have any more pictures of Bradley and me, or of Bradley and the children, or of Bradley and the dogs. That one photo was the only evidence of what our life was like in the good times—when Bradley was sober.

The family moved forward with their plans for Bradley's celebration, but I didn't go. It wasn't because I wasn't invited or wanted or accepted by them. I didn't go because they would not acknowledge who I had been to the one they were celebrating, and I could not stand for any more lies in my life. I was the best for Bradley. I still am. I celebrate him every day I am alive and not dead in the ground. I celebrate him every waking hour and moment, down to the very second. I celebrate him by continuing to love his family. I am happy that I can really talk about Bradley in such an honest, loving, and powerful way now. The truth about his addiction and illness set me free to love him, by celebrating him the right way and most of all, unconditionally.

From that moment forward, I found my footing and made some boundaries. I never once again explained to anyone who I had been to Bradley. I let so many people go from my life. I shook the leaves off. The best part? I don't lose any sleep over it. I pray for those people to find what I believe they lack: hope.

I may have not been represented at the celebration of life, but I do find some humour in it all. It makes me giggle seeing how I believe God works. They used the one picture I had taken of him—that same one I had been brave enough to take when he was wearing his billiards team shirt. There he was, looking over his shoulder as he traced the outlines for the wolf pattern circling an eight ball. I remember he was criticizing the shading and line work at the time. Beside the photo was the urn filled with his ashes, the very one the children and I designed together. I giggle because we were all there really. There were traces of us everywhere, celebrating us—celebrating Bradley.

I see my past romantic relationships as branches on my tree. In search of intimacy, I would re-shape myself to be exactly what those men wanted. Being liked was more important to me than showing my true self. The first branches to break on my tree represented these relationships, which were based on a lie. Those branches were flimsy and when they eventually broke, it was painful. I have been walked out on, abandoned, rejected, and left empty. Some of them tried to put the blame on me and convince me that the reason they left was because the love I had given them wasn't enough. Each one of them took a chunk of my innocence and left a permanent scar. I've since realized that there's no sense in changing who I am to please someone. Now I'm looking for a man who will accept me for who I am and love me for *me*—purple hair, tattoos, and all.

For now, I am an amputated tree with no leaves. What I do have are some deep, strong roots. While I have had some difficult relationships, I am fortunate to have some special people in my life. These people have integrity, wisdom, and true love for me. They have made me strong and have provided me with the resilience I have needed to persevere in the hardest times of my life.

I refer to one of my roots as "my heart." She is the epitome of compassion and the very essence of patience. This woman has mastered the meaning of the word "love," and she loves unconditionally. To me, she is the most beautiful woman I have ever seen, and I fall in love with her every day of my life. My life would have no meaning without her steady embrace and warmth.

I cried in pain for so many days and nights when Bradley died. Only she knew the depth of my love for him. She witnessed all the suffering during our young adult lives. I would often talk to her about him and express my need for my attachment to him.

She saw my heartache decades before his death. Even then she told me, "Elisha, if he can't see your worth as I do then he doesn't deserve you."

In the aftermath of his death, she was the first to hold me and feed me, the first to come and bathe me. She looked after my children as if they were her own. She stood by me as people came to my door to pay their respects. She allowed me space to cry and used her own hand to wipe my tears. And she protected me. When someone would try to take advantage of me in my vulnerable state, she would say, "I don't think this is the time, nor the place. Elisha needs her space to heal surrounded by the ones who love her." She knew not to leave me alone with the vultures.

She was the one who was with me when I heard the banging on the second night after Bradley passed. Until that day, I always thought I was the stronger one. I had never seen such strength in her before. When I woke up early, panicking over the sound, I began to pace back and forth, searching for answers and wondering if I had gone insane. "Did you hear that sound?" I breathlessly asked her.

"Tell me about the sound you heard," she said, her voice sweet and calm.

She never gave me a sad look but instead listened intently to my words. It was never a question of whether she believed me or not. She looked at me with her big green eyes, smiled softly, and held my hand. Her heart was open to accept all that I was and all that I have ever been. She has stood by my side from the very beginning. My heart isn't complete without her. Our hearts beat together as one.

I have another root who insists I call her "girlfriend" in public. She believes that term describes who she truly is to me. She reminds me to laugh and have fun while I am still young and beautiful. My girlfriend is a root who acknowledges hardship and the true meaning of perseverance. She sees me for who I truly am, regardless of what others think.

She is always the life of any party or celebration. She's a secretly competitive gift giver and loves to make others laugh with her jokes. She loves to show off her creative side with her handmade skirts and dresses. She keeps me real—authentic—and puts my mind at ease. Her voice soothes me when she sings and comforts me when she talks. There is never a dull moment with this wonderful person around.

Her heart was devastated when Bradley died. Seeing me in such pain shattered a part of her completely. "When something happens to you, I feel your pain so much more," she told me. My grief traumatized her because I came from her and carry her soul in me. To my surprise, she wouldn't allow me to forget my courage or stay still in a state of wallowing. She told me, "He deserves every tear, so cry and cry some more; but when you're done crying, pick up your feet. You have a life to live!"

She has provided unwavering guidance and has persistently pushed me to find my best self through the hardest times of my life, reminding me that no one will fight for the life I want so it has to be me fighting for it. She often displays her affection for me by reciting all I have accomplished in such a short time. She has watched me persevere, standing in support of all my decisions. She has always been there to catch me if I fall and tell me, "Try again!"

We both have lost so much in our lives, but we are committed to living openly so that not a single second is wasted. To prepare me, she made me a "Girlfriend Emergency Kit." It was filled with little fidget toys and other items for distraction, and she included instructions for every single one. Her sense of humour keeps me alive. She told me, "Laughter may heal the soul, but my laughter is the only one of its kind!"

I have another vital root who I call "my rock." I can honestly say I would not be the woman I am today without this man's discipline. I have looked up to him my whole life. He is my best friend and companion. I will never lie to him in fear of losing his trust and I love him deeply. We connect on a spiritual level that there aren't enough words to explain. We are one another's firm hand at times; at other times, we offer each other a soft compassionate voice.

I have never heard him cry as hard as he did the day that Bradley died, his head over Bradley's silent heart. I held Bradley in my arms while he wept over him. He loved Bradley like he was his own son. My rock has always been strong for me but in this moment he couldn't be. He and I managed to come together with love always leading the way. He has never seen me so broken, and this only broke him more. Seeing me suffering in such misery took a piece of his heart too. He knew everything about Bradley and me. He knew what I had been trying to do with this man all along. Any time doubt would come in for the kill, my rock became a good and fair judge, explaining the truth clearly using his wisdom. He would hold me in his arms and remind me of who I am, of what is to come, and to stay on the path provided for me. He taught me never to take criticism from someone you wouldn't get advice from.

I have never seen such leadership before in my life. It's not because of his riches or good fortune. It's not even a result of his deeds. He is a leader because I know who he follows and together we have such a passion for it; it's a whole-hearted effort that drives both of us in everything we do in life and brings us closer to one another. Without this man, I would have been dead a long time ago. He taught me the most important thing to survive and live in joy with the world. He has disciplined me in love, perfect love, always accepting my crooked ways and heart. It was his love and his faith that taught me to love the unlovable. He helped me understand what it meant to love Bradley. He taught me to remember the promise of what lies ahead. I swear he can predict the future. With wrinkles on his face and a smile bigger than ever he declares, "I am excited for you!" We understand where this comes from and he, as my rock, stands firmly to ground my whole being on this earth. My favourite thing he does is grab me for the strongest hug I know and say, "I am so proud of you, Elisha."

I refer to another one of my roots as "the poet." For years, I have stood back and watched him from a distance, never knowing how he truly felt about me. There is such a difference in age between us. When we were growing up, we couldn't relate to each other on many topics, but I loved observing how free he was. I settled down too quickly, before I truly knew myself. He, on the other hand, has done everything with purpose, driven to explore himself as a man and travel anywhere and everywhere he wanted. He has never believed in settling. I have grown so fond of him. He has shared his failures with me, which I have always found quite comical. I won't hear from him for months at a time, but then he visits with stories of his adventures. He's seen so much of the world, and I have lived through him in a way. He inspires me.

Shortly after Bradley's passing, he did three things that changed my life and made me want to live more fully. The first thing he did was offer me a new perspective—a new way to manifest what I want in my life. We were hiking together, and we started talking about our lives. All his life he has set goals. He has made it his mission to achieve them. He has pursued everything he wanted. That day, he politely told me what he thought my biggest problem was: I expected the men in my life to make my life happen for me. I expected them to make me happy and fulfill my dreams. He said that I have lived for them and carried out their wishes for their lives while ignoring my own. He told me that he loved me dearly, but that I had been wrong to ever put that on a man's shoulders.

He said what I needed to hear to start living my life for me. To make his point, he freely and without hesitation offered to help me financially while I was on leave. This was the second thing he did, and it was very powerful. He taught me the true meaning of a stress-free life: the security of financial independence and the power it gave me to create my own happiness. He changed my thinking. From that moment on, as he put it, I would "not live to work, but rather I would work to live my life."

When we see each other, we both glow with excitement. I remember one time when he really made an impression on me. He was signing Christmas cards and mentioned a single man's name. Half joking, I asked, "Is he single?"

"Yes, but he isn't your type," he replied immediately.

I gave him a questioning look, thinking to myself, "As if he knows my type." But once he started describing the individual, I realized he was right. The guy was not my type at all. Then out of nowhere, he said something I will never forget: "I am saving you!"

When he said that, he made me feel on top of the world and safe, because I realized that he will always be looking out for me. It was the best compliment he's ever given me. I was so touched that I cried when I heard his words. I can't wait for the right man to come into my life so he can meet this man. He has taught me to stop looking to be inspired and instead, to be the inspiration I am looking for. He has many sayings, but this is one of my favourites: "People don't care what you know, until they know how much you care."

The third thing he did was to write a poem for me. He read it to me on Christmas Eve, 2021, out loud in front of his girlfriend and their golden retriever, Finlay, in the house they all share. The poem expresses all that he is: his sense of humour, his honesty, and most of all, the fact that he really cares to know who I am. With this poem, he truly inspired such a feeling of self-worth in me. He gave me hope.

'Twas the night before Christmas,
When all through the hall,
Not a creature was stirring,
Not even Finlay with his ball.

The girlfriend nestled all snug in her bed,
With visions of eagle eggs being eaten in her head,
When out in the driveway,
There arose such a clatter,
I sprang from the couch,
To see what was the matter.

Away to the window I waddled like a hag,
I poked my finger between the blinds, pulled down, let them sag.
The moon on the breast of another foot of snow,
Gave the thought of more shoveling, good grief, Oh NO!

When what to my wondering eyes should appear?
But a Jeep in my driveway, Elisha is here!
With a leisurely smile and lovely purple hair,
I whisked her inside, the temps were unfair.

She tore off her scarf and tossed it to the floor,
She shouted, "I don't want to deal with this shit anymore!
Fuck Dasher, Dancer, Prancer and Vixen,
Screw Comet, Cupid, Donner and Blitzen."

We put the kettle on to pour her some tea,
We sat her on the couch, put on "The Dundee."
We gave her a hug and held on to her tight.
Time spent with true people is never a fee,
Christmas is you, Sarah, Finlay, and as well, me.

The next root I want to tell you about is my legacy; he is my "man of the house." Sometimes I think I have no right to laugh, and yet laugh I do, now more than ever in my life. I smile every day just thinking about him and how in love I am with him. He knows how to keep me in check by tackling me to the ground when my stress levels are high. He never takes me seriously and is always arguing with me in his goofy stubborn manner. When I am disciplining him, I sometimes have to look away so he doesn't see me smile. It never works. He adores me more than any other man ever has. He runs me a bath with candles often, making sure to ask in his smart-ass way, "Am I making you a tea this evening or grabbing a bottle of wine?" The way I look at him determines the answer.

He is so protective of me. I am given curfews and told to eat well and to "chill the fuck out." He makes fun of me during baseball season, yelling, "Run faster! Come on, Linda!" Anytime someone compliments my hair and tattoos, he puts me in check by reminding me, "It's the inside that counts, Mother." He writes me loving letters about our relationship. He often tells me I am his best friend and the strongest person he knows. He made me a promise for when I am old, grey, and shitting in a diaper. He has to wipe my ass and make sure I still have purple hair and white roses in my room at all times. Almost every day, he makes sure I tell him, "You're my favourite!"

He has never been the same after seeing his mother so broken. He journals just like Bradley did. One evening I came across one of his entries. He titled it "The Day I Became a Man." He misses his best friend and father figure. He made a promise to always look after me and his sister and actually gave *himself* the title "man of the house." In his writing, I can hear Bradley's voice. Their intelligence is equal. He promised Bradley that he would not let his mother be with another man unless he saw that man return love to her on the same level. The most important lesson for a young man is to learn about love. I am glad he got to witness what true love looks like although there are things I wish he had not seen.

I have one more root to describe. I have too many nicknames for this individual: "Do-ga-loug," "Chicken Liver," "Freckle Fart," "Snuggle Bear," "Turkey Butt," "Miss Muffet," my little "Hay Hay." Watching my every move, she carefully creates her own likeness of me within herself. We tend to argue more and disagree often on who is more beautiful. She wins every battle with her freckle-covered face and her blue eyes, deep as the night sky. Her peers and teachers at school tell me she has the biggest heart but that they are impressed with her thoughts most of all. "Hailey is a deep thinker," they tell me. She always prays for me and comes to my side when the tears flow, kissing them away. She has confessed that she is in love with me, and I told her the same. She told me I am a "badass." When I inquired as to what she meant, she said, "Mom, when you walk into any room, everyone knows who you are!"

She was the closest to Bradley, closer even than me. Their relationship was pure and innocent, and she was always kind and loving towards him. She trusted him and called him "Dad" from the age of three. In her eyes, he was perfect. Her bond with him was so strong, I don't think any other man will ever be as close to her.

Many difficulties arose for her after his death. She couldn't understand it and shouted repeatedly, "Why him?!" She never saw the ugliness of the disease and illness that imprisoned him. Now, she draws pictures of Bradley in heaven, making sure to always add his brown goatee and frizzy curly hair; in the pictures, he is always saying, "I love you, baby girl!" Those were the last words he said to her. She has lost a part of her, and she is always aware of that pain in her heart. We come together frequently to heal, share time and space, and hold one another's pain. She often demands that I sing her to sleep so she can drift away and dream of seeing her dad again. She reminds me to stay humble and keep space for my pain. She knows when to make me laugh and when to let me cry. She knows when to make me tea and when to hand me an ice cream. If she feels like nothing is working, she keeps me real and honest by telling me, "Mom, for my honesty, you are kinda being a sucky baby!" Whenever I lose my mind with stress or my anger gets the best of me, she can sweep me up with her compassion; but she can also be quite strict and to the point when she tells me, "With all due respect Mom, you're kinda being a bitch!"

I am never allowed to doubt who I am as a mother to her and her brother. In her eyes, I am perfect and never beyond repair. She is my most resilient root.

Perhaps that is where we can be with the Holy Spirit intimately. Come to the realization that whatever happens is meant to happen, that we should celebrate the beauty that is. That is the grand design.

(From Bradley's journal, April 2021)

SIXTEEN

I can see myself sitting and typing away at the computer, knowing full well this is the final chapter; this book is coming to its conclusion. In the process, I have returned to each chapter finding any excuse to write more about him. On my first Christmas without him, I was sick with strep throat and alone. I sat there staring at the blank pages. I couldn't stop crying. I couldn't finish what I had started. I didn't want it to end. I didn't want this final chapter, his legacy, to leave me.

Writing this book was hard. Most days, I felt like I'd been hit by a truck. I was nauseous at the idea of publishing this manuscript. I was afraid to take a stand. I wonder if I have said enough about love. Have I represented him properly? Will people understand the love we gave to one another? Is he watching? Is he proud of me? What if people hate me for what I have written about him? What if, in the end, I don't have the courage to expose the truth about this man? Is Bradley at peace with my words? Will his legacy endure? Will his story and his words be remembered? Will they give hope to those who suffer?

We don't always get to choose what happens to us, but we do

get to choose what we do next. I have finally reached a state of acceptance: the final stage of the grief process. I give permission for people to know the truth—his truth. It has never been about "making it." It has always been about what this book can give: the inspiration to see things differently, feel more deeply, and act more courageously. So often today, I witness acts of cruelty perpetrated by people with calloused hearts and minds. Harsh judgements are often placed on those who are broken and barely able to fight the fight of their lives. Bradley was one of them. He deserves to be seen through my eyes and heart.

While many abandoned him, I stayed. I've heard some people say, "Don't cross oceans for people who won't cross a puddle for you." To that, I say, "No! *Do* cross oceans for people." Love all people—no conditions attached. Don't spend time wondering whether they are worthy. Cross that ocean. Climb that mountain. Life and love are not what you gain; they are about what you *give!*

I give him to you. Our story is no longer a secret. This book is a testimony, and I am your witness. Take my pain and tell others there is still hope. I want people to understand the disease behind the man—a *good* man. Addiction is a medical condition, *not* a choice. Bradley was trapped in a battle he had no chance of winning. He persevered for as long as he could, and he suffered greatly. I want to shine a light on the illness that destroyed him but also show that we can build a new lifestyle free of pain and full of the promise of new chapters. Changing people's thinking is my goal.

I hope that by writing about my experience, I can help someone else whose loved one is fighting this disease. If that's you, open the door. Make sure you know how cared for and loved you are. Your heartache is also mine. I want to validate your feelings.

My struggle has ended, but I am here on the sidelines, relating to all you're going through without judgement. I hope my voice will give you courage and strength when you need it most. As Mr. Blunt told me once, "My opinions are well thought out and free of judgement."

What motivated me to write this book? Why tell others about my experience? Honestly, it was a way to coach myself through my grief. Bradley's death devastated me. I never intended anyone to read this. Writing is what I do when I need to be honest about how I feel. Sometimes it's the only way for me to know my own feelings. I have to write in order to see them and to be seen for who I truly am, without lies or secrets. I find it a lot easier to write the truth than to say it out loud. No one can take that away from me or tell me that I am wrong. My words are right. My words are fucking right because they are mine. This is my testimony. To have courage in this world is to have something to say out of love. I truly love him and that will never change. I had to write this book to explain what true love really is and to show my readers how it resides within them. A simple act of love has the power to change the outcome of any situation. I wrote about what I cared most for in this world—what I was afraid of. I wrote about what I loved. I chased after it. I didn't back away from what is right just because it was hard. I planted my feet and stood firm.

The question is, where are you going to plant your feet?

I never felt guilty for writing this book, but I have to admit that at times, I lacked courage. I've been living in fear—fear of how others might react to my truth, fear of their judgement. I feared exposing Bradley. It was my secret for so long; I dared not set it free or deal with the consequences: the wrath of others. I had someone once ask me what finally gave me the courage to write the book. "Bradley's death," I responded.

I had been living under his control and in fear of him for years. His anger and abuse, under the influence of his disease, left me weak and wanting to hide. After his death, I felt safe to share my story, and his, in love. Still, I doubted writing, and I know what I have written about isn't easy to digest. A dear friend of mine reminded me of my greater purpose in telling this story when she told me, "Your words will touch so many people." When I questioned how she knew this, she replied, "Because of your story, I now know what true love is."

I know this story might hurt the people who don't understand the truth. I would tell anyone who is upset by this book to go back and just read the title again. You don't need to go any further than that to understand my relationship with Bradley. I hope you will decide to choose mercy over judgement. I want to be heard, but I won't shoot sunshine up anyone's ass. Sometimes the truth is not pretty. My life with Bradley was incredibly ugly at times. At other times, it was utterly beautiful. Throughout it all, I was completely in love with him. That is the complicated truth of this experience.

Bradley never knew how much I loved him here on Earth because he couldn't see past his own pain. His suffering hardened his heart and made him believe he was unlovable, but it was just a reflection of his disease. He became cruel as a result, and only hated himself more for it. The cycle replayed itself, and he was pulled further and further down. He could not win.

As I write this, I can hear him say, "Don't be afraid, my love. It was my time!" Bradley made peace with God. He was never able to thank me for giving him a chance at a good life, but one day we will see each other again and I know he will. Death is a part of life; no one can escape it. For a short while, I was in

Bradley's life and did the best I could to improve it and to show him the possibility of what he could become. I believe we are all meant to be in charge of our own destiny. We have to do the best with what God gives us. When Bradley died, I lost such a huge part of myself; he was my world, the man I loved, and now he's gone. Not a day goes by that I don't picture what might have been if we'd had more time. Bradley had his whole life ahead of him. He had so much beautiful potential. I wonder what my destiny is now.

One night while I was cleaning the salon, our song came on and I started to dance slowly. I held up my arms and closed my eyes; I could feel him with me there in my embrace. "Are you going to let me lead, Linda?" a soft voice asked. I giggled, imagining myself standing on his toes so he could lead the way. Taking my hand softly in his, he led. Right then it dawned on me. I was dancing with a ghost. Bradley had to pass away for me to really know how deep my love for him was, that he was my very soul and thought. Everything I am is a reflection of him. And now, in rest and peace, he can finally see how much I love him. Free from his disease and suffering, at last he sees me. I opened my eyes, looked up, and said, "Now you know more than ever how much I love you!" I felt his spirit hold mine and receive with joy the knowledge that he is so deeply loved.

To return to the question "Do I have peace?" Yes. I do! I now have complete and final peace. It's hard to let go, isn't it? But that is life; what can I tell you? A person must deal with the truth of the pain that resides in them in order to heal. Without the truth, you'll never heal. Without faith, there is no hope. Bradley, near the end of his life, started journaling and writing about his greatest passion: Jesus. His faith softened his heart; he knew he was forgiven. In times of hardship, trials, and tests, Bradley fell into drinking. Triggers would send him spiraling down. He didn't know how to ask for help, but I know his faith helped him.

People always say if you love something you have to let it go. I always thought that was such bullshit until I held Bradley in my arms that day. Nothing else mattered to me in that moment—just him. He was and continues to be everything to me. I hold on to that moment in remembrance of him; it's in my mind every day.

I don't know what comes next, but I don't regret a thing. Despite all that I went through and did for this man, I am happy in all that I've done. I gave him the greatest gift: I saw his worth and gave him my love and time while he was alive. I led him to something far greater than the both of us.

Now I need to live *my* life. It is hard to describe how I feel, but I am ok. I still struggle to put it into words, but if I had to, I'd say I feel warm, like I'm under a blanket. I know something bigger than me is coming, something I wouldn't have chosen for myself. To be honest with you, I am so scared, but I have to believe there is a greater purpose. If one person's life is changed by our story, it will all be worth it.

There is one question I've been asking myself: *can* I live without him? I was never meant to. Bradley is with me everywhere I go; everywhere I look, I see him. He is right here with me. We're touching heaven together in spirit. The time that we had together was too short. I have faced many difficulties, but I have overcome each of them. Some days are harder than others, but I made a decision long ago. It was when I was fifteen years old, to be exact. I chose to love him. Every single day. I will never see Bradley again while I walk this earth, but I wake up every morning and feel his presence next to me. I have so much joy knowing that I made the choice to love him, and this brings me comfort.

I will love him until the end of time. He wasn't perfect, but he is not unlovable. He is worthy.

Bradley believed otherwise and never truly understood his worth. He was made to believe he needed to be without fault in order to be loved. He was wrong. All the proof he needed was before him. He just needed to look up and see me standing there. I was by his side until the end. I am tired of pretending and I cannot continue acting. I do love every aspect of this wretched man, even the parts that he believed were too dark and shameful. Every scar, flaw, and imperfection, I loved. He may have thought he was too damaged and broken to allow himself to be loved. However, he could have chosen differently: he could have chosen love. That should never be up to anyone else. Ever. It was only ever up to him. Nothing else matters other than his heart, and how he needed to fill it.

The best thing Bradley let into his life and his heart was me. He gave his heart to me and allowed me to love him perfectly. Bradley died with his eyes closed but his heart was open. I believe this was a miracle. I believe I was put in his path, chosen, and sent to soften his heart just enough to prepare the way to meet his maker.

I imagine dying is the hardest thing one has to go through. You leave behind so many who love you. Do I understand why Bradley isn't here anymore? Not completely. I do understand that my life is full. I feel rich and I am proud of who I became because of this man. Not many understood my willingness to walk into fire with him, but that is what unconditional love is: sacrifice. I was given this privilege, and I am stronger today because of it.

I do not have all of the answers. But I do know this: my life is not full despite the disappointments; it's full *because* of them. I had my miracle. It was falling in love. As the character Melissa says in the movie *I Still Believe*, "suffering doesn't destroy faith, it refines it." It is worth trusting even when we can't see. I see Bradley. He is safe and walks bravely into the light; he has found a peace that I cannot describe in words. Waiting for me to join him one day, I hear him say, "When you're ready, shine for both of us, my love."

Linda: 8; Bradley: 9.
(Bradley: "I win! I made it to heaven before you!")

I made a promise before I started this book that the very last part would be Bradley's final journal entry. I hope every single one of you who have read my book are driven to acknowledge what love is. I give you his words, from his heart; this is his truth, and it took courage for him to put pen to paper.

Are you lonely? Does it feel like your world is falling to pieces? Do you carry guilt, shame, regret, anger, or sadness in your conscience? Do you feel like you can't escape yesterday and dread what will come tomorrow? Do you feel stuck and confused about who you are or what your life purpose is? Do you find that no matter what you do or try, you're only maintaining your existence and not experiencing any change or growth? Finances in rough shape? The list could go on and on; everyone has struggles in some aspects of their life. Don't fool yourself into thinking that you're alone in your pursuit of happiness or that your neighbour lives in the paradise you see on the surface or in social media. We all fall short, desire more, fail in relationships or at work. We all have internal strife we deal with whether that's family, mental health, disability, addictions, hatred, fear, or trauma. Our struggles are relative to ourselves not others. Your issue is relevant. Remember this always. You are worthy of seeking help and searching for guidance. Are you searching for forgiveness but cannot find it in yourself or someone else? I live a good life. I was raised above the poverty line and spoiled. I have travelled all over North America; I have a good job and family to support me when I fail. I have never gone without anything that I need. I say these things because it is important for you to know who I am and how much security I have.

I have not hit rock bottom if you compare my struggles with yours, but my issues are still relevant and matter. I am worthy of love, joy, happiness, and forgiveness despite the horrible things that I have done, and the things done to me. I cannot truly understand what you have been through, or what you have done and how you feel. I can empathize, but that is never really enough for me when I pour my heart out to someone. Is it enough for you?

The reason I say you are worthy is because for a very long time, even until today, I struggled to remember and accept that *I* am worthy. I am enough. This fear of not deserving forgiveness and the shame of failing over and over again kept me from turning my heart to Jesus Christ. So many people have it worse than me; how could I ask for more? I doubted that Jesus wanted someone as sinful as myself in His kingdom. What about everyone else that has issues worse than mine? I considered myself unworthy because I was following the world; I was following my logic and not the true understanding of "the way."

This thinking, coupled with my own ego and education, left me doubting if there even was a God. I was angry, ashamed, guilty, sinful, fearful, and in pain. I still am. But I am worthy of His love and mercy. You are worthy of His love and mercy.

I am an infant in my spiritual journey. I am just beginning to learn about my heavenly Father's life and about the sacrifice God made when He gave His son over to man so that we may all be forgiven for our past and shed tears for the worries of tomorrow. Perhaps forgiveness is understandable but given how I explained who I was it may seem easy to you for me to shed my worries for tomorrow. Truthfully yes, it may be easier, but it doesn't mean I am not worthy. Remember, we are all relative to ourselves. You may be a small cub with one arrow in your back and me the large alpha with twenty arrows in my back. Does this mean one or the other is unworthy of healing? Pain is relative. We all need healing regardless of who we are. We are enough. You are enough.

Open your heart and shed the world of man and you will find how much more love and mercy Jesus has for you. He says, "You are worthy of me."

—Bradley Kempster

"It's supposed to be hard. If it wasn't hard, everyone would do it. The hard is what makes it great."

Jimmy Dugan in *A League of Their Own*.

EPILOGUE

Playa del Carmen, Mexico
December 16, 2022

I have always wanted a life that is full; that way, I will have something to share with those I love. As my feet sink down into this blanket of soft, fluffy, white-beige sand, I realize I have created this life. The smell of salty air fills my nose as I hear the waves crashing down on the rocks. The sun rises over the water, sparkling down on the bright green and shallow shores of the Caribbean Sea.

Ahead of me, I see myself. She is an innocent version of me. Her freckles glow and her sun-kissed hair shines as she runs eagerly to get her feet in the water. I smile as I look down to see a young man picking up shells, first cupping them in his hands and then throwing them into the ocean. He's grown tall and slender. His blond hair has been bleached by the sun; his skin smells of warmth and copal incense. He smiles his bright dashing smile and takes me into his deep blue eyes. Towering over me, he wraps one arm around my shoulders and asks, "Are you ready, Mom?" He calls his sister over as she races from a wave.

I take the glass toothpaste jar from my pocket. Inside is a precious powder, one that I have kept a secret until now. I pour some of the light grey dust carefully into my son's hands and give the glass jar with the rest of the remains to my daughter.

Bradley always wanted to travel and see the world with the loves of his life. Now he is here with us, smuggled across the border and into another country. Disguised as toothpaste powder to make the journey, he now smells of peppermint oil. He would have loved that. "Oh Linda," he would have said. I thought it was clever. My only fear was the children mistaking it for actual toothpaste powder and brushing their teeth with Bradley's dust and bones. I couldn't tell them what I was carrying with us when we were travelling. It was too risky. But now they know; they understand why this jar is so valuable and what lies within.

Tanner walks a few steps forward with Bradley's ashes in hand and baseball throws into the wind. The dust immediately blows back into his face, and he starts trying to spit the dust out of his mouth. Immediately I grab my stomach as the pain of my laugher unleashes. Typical teenager, always in such a rush! That's karma for you.

"I definitely swallowed Dad!" Tanner sputters.

Hailey is now on her knees, her eyes watering over her brother's pathetic display at our celebration of life. Her laughter fills the air and deep down I know Bradley planned this.

"What do you think Bradley's lesson is to you right now, Tanner?" I ask.

"Slow down!" he answers, without a second thought.

We all started crying and laughing together. Tanner's sense of humour is identical to Bradley's in so many ways. Hailey rises to her feet and pinches a small amount of Bradley in her tiny fingers. Delicately rubbing her fingers together as if she was seasoning with salt, she gently releases Bradley. She repeats this process four times, each time more powerful than the first. Tears are falling from her face and mine. This is the space she creates for him in her own way and in her heart. I dare not go to her; she needs this. She is speaking but I can't hear her very well. I can just make out the words she has put together for him: "Thank you for loving me. I am proud to be your daughter."

She comes to me, and she gives me the look. Our eyes meet. She grabs my hand and pours the rest of him into my palm. Tanner touches his head to my head and places a hand on his sister. The three of us form a triangle united and bound in love for this man we will hold forever and will never forget. They gently send me forward and I walk to the shoreline alone with him. I look back at my children who wait patiently for me, and I am awed by the respect they give, not to a mother, but to a woman who holds a part of her heart and her world in her hand. I start shaking, questioning myself and terrified of this moment: time to let go!

I slowly bend down; my knees are so weak, and I feel as if I am about to fall. Reaching my hands down into the water, I squeeze them so tight to hang on to him. Is this what is best for me? Best for us? I close my eyes, feel the wind blow my hair, and with it I hear these words of comfort:

"You will never let go; you were never meant to. I am always going to be with you and a part of you. Celebrate my life, every moment, every second of every minute of each day. Time to wake up, my love!"

Open your heart and shed the world of man and you will find how much more love and mercy Jesus has for you. He says, "You are WORTHY of me."

Bradley Kempster

ACKNOWLEDGEMENTS

I could not have survived, let alone write this book, without the help of my friends and family. These people never gave up on me. They stood by me and showered me with love and support and gave me hope during my darkest time.

I want to thank:

- my father Peter, for teaching me the only thing that has saved me: faith.

- my mother Glenda, for her endless compassion and her strength that has lifted me up.

- my sister Ruth, for always believing in me and feeding me.

- my brother Sam, for his leadership and his poetry.

- my son Tanner and my daughter Hailey, for giving me a reason to live and be the best mother I can possibly be. I am full of so much love and joy because of you.

- Kyle, for being a wonderful man and father.

- Meghan, for being a strong fortress for us and a beautiful mother.

- the children's father's extended family, for all the strength and support.

- Anthony, for loving me and never leaving my side.

- my dear cousin Amanda, for never forsaking me and standing by me.

- my cousin Greg, for his wise words and being there for Tanner and Hailey.

- my sister-in-law Allison, for listening to me and holding me up.

- my sisters at heart, Sara and Janine, who put me in my place more than once with love and perseverance.

- my "other mothers", Morria and Marni, for inspiring me.

- Shauna, for reminding me of who I am without all the bullshit.

- Sydney, for never doubting me for a second and always guarding my space.

- Courtnay, for her healing energy.

- Jenaie and Jamie, for bringing me into their family.

– Delaney, for holding my every tear.

– Zack and Austin, for all the laughs.

– Jessy, for your sense of truth and twisted humour.

– Stacie, for the very powerful hugs.

– my dear friend Chunk, for the years of support and
  friendship.

– my extended family, the Whytes, Curries, and Crosbys,
  for their love.

– all my clients, who stood by me and supported my business
  and my family. Thank you for the love you gave us.

– complete strangers, who knew and loved Bradley as a boy,
  for coming and giving my family support.

I will never forget what you have done for me and my family. You
got me through the hardest time in my life. I owe you everything.

Made in the USA
Columbia, SC
28 September 2023